SOLO
FOOD

JANNEKE VREUGDENHIL

SOLO FOOD

72 RECIPES FOR YOU ALONE

CONTENTS

10   Introduction
20   7 tips for the solo chef
22   Your very own golden pantry

QUICK FIX

28   A kind of pisto Manchego
30   Spicy lamb pittas with hummus & garlicky yoghurt
32   Miso soup with noodles, shiitake mushrooms, spinach & an egg
34   Ridiculously easy spaghetti caprese
35   Frittata with red onion, baby kale & goat's cheese
38   Griddled white tuna with cucumber, avocado & ginger salad
40   Tagliatelle with prawns & smoky whisky–tomato sauce
42   Lemon couscous with salmon & cherry tomatoes
44   Salad of butter beans, tinned tuna & shaved fennel
46   Good old steak sandwich

SMART COOKING

50	Baked sweet potato with olives, feta & chilli
53	Sweet potato soup with coconut & fresh coriander
54	Soft polenta with mushrooms & spinach
56	Polenta pizza with blistered cherry tomatoes & anchovies
60	Mash with baby kale & chorizo
62	Patatas a lo pobre
64	Warm lentil salad with grilled goat's cheese
66	Spicy lentil soup with yoghurt & rocket
68	Cod in ginger–tomato sauce with gremolata & rice
71	Best-ever fried rice
72	Chinese egg noodles with steak & oyster sauce
74	Cold noodle salad with cucumber & sashimi salmon

NETFLIX DINNER

78	Quinotto with fennel, almonds & avocado
80	Gnocchi with broad beans, brown butter & crispy sage
82	Quick aubergine & lamb curry with warm naan
84	Pasta aglio olio my way
85	Green curry with chicken & peas
86	Warm salad of baby potatoes & peppered mackerel
88	Spaghetti with cherry tomatoes, nutmeg & ricotta
90	Orecchiette with Tenderstem broccoli, anchovies & fennel seed
93	Courgette soup with tarragon
96	Bowl of rice with Chinesey vegetables

FREEZE YOUR FAVOURITES

100   Chilli con everything

102   All-round chicken soup

104   Comforting little casseroles

106   Roasted squash & carrot soup

110   Pasta sauce with fresh sausage & fennel seed

111   Pork loin stewed with red wine & bay leaves

112   Marcella's sugo

114   Pesto at your fingertips

116   Ratatouille

118   Surinamese masala chicken

120   Basic nasi goreng (Indonesian fried rice)

CLASSICS FOR ONE

124   Steak Béarnaise with chips & salad

126   Sea bass in a salt crust

128   Cheat's pizza Margherita

130   Solo chicken with rosemary & Roseval potatoes

131   Cassoulet

132   10-minute pho

136   Caesar salad with crispy pancetta & avocado

138   Lamb chops with red wine & thyme sauce & green beans

139   Steak tartare

140   Risotto ai funghi

142   Too-good-to-share cheese fondue

BE SWEET TO YOURSELF

146 Blackberry mess
148 Instant mango–coconut ice cream
150 Lemon mug cake
152 Warm apple tartlet with vanilla ice cream
153 Coffee–ricotta parfait
154 La mousse au chocolat pour toi
158 Rosemary–honey figs with Gorgonzola
160 A fantastic raspberry dessert
160 Pear–yoghurt swirl
162 Tiramisu for one, please!

SOLO TREATS

166 Oatmeal congee
168 Parma ham–Taleggio toastie de luxe
171 Scrambled eggs, griddled asparagus
     & salmon on toast
172 Stir-fried prawns with harissa mayo
174 Potato gratin with a whole load of cheese
176 Calf's liver sans etiquette
178 Party for one
180 Oysters, Champagne & a good book

182 A word of thanks
184 Index

INTRODUCTION

The high point

On the kitchen counter are a steak, two lumpy potatoes and a head of lettuce. My evening meal. I slice off a chunk of butter and drop it into the pan. Plop. Turn on the hob, sizzling sounds. The butter bubbles furiously and then, slowly but surely, the foam dies down and a hush descends over the pan. White flakes form on the bottom of the pan. I grip the handle and pour the contents on to a piece of kitchen paper that I've placed in a sieve. The glass measuring jug fills with clear yellow liquid. My laptop is on the counter, too, opened out and tuned in to Spotify. My fingertips conjure up the sounds of John Coltrane. I rinse out the pan and pour in a splash of white wine. An equal amount of vinegar. I peel and finely chop a shallot, pluck the pointed leaves from two sprigs of tarragon. I fill a glass with wine, and as I drink from it, I let the liquid in the pan evaporate until there's no more than a tablespoon and a half left. I peel the potatoes, slice them into thick matchsticks, rinse them under the tap, then dry them in a tea towel. I put a frying pan on the hob, add a splash of oil, then the potatoes and cover with a lid. It's a mild April day, the promise of summer, and I open the kitchen window. Coltrane blows his *My Favorite Things*, and I sing along. First softly, then louder. Louder and louder and more

off-key. No one can hear me. I'm alone. I'm making myself steak Béarnaise with chips and salad. *And then I don't feel so bad.*

I wash and dry the lettuce. Mix together a dressing of mustard, red wine vinegar, olive oil, pepper and salt. Hot and sharp. Probably too hot and too sharp for any guest who might taste it, but just the way I like it. I strain the reduced wine into a bowl. Crack an egg, separate out the white and drop the yolk into the bowl. Rinse out the pan again, fill it with water and bring it to the boil. Place the bowl over the pan. I start to whisk and then very gradually add the clarified butter in a thin stream. My finger glides through the custardy sauce and moves towards my mouth. Mmmm. A squeeze of lemon, a sprinkle of salt, then some chervil and a little more tarragon. Take the lid off the potatoes, turn up the heat. Sputtering oil, sizzling chips. Coarse salt on the steak. Griddle pan on the hob. When the air above the pan begins to quiver, I place the meat on the steel ridges. One minute only – I like it bloody – then the other side. Beautiful black stripes burned into the dark red meat.

Man, do I love Coltrane. While the meat is resting, I hum as I look for my favourite plate, a flea-market find made of white porcelain

and decorated with delicate blue blossom sprigs, a dragonfly, a butterfly and birds. I get a napkin from the cabinet, grab some cutlery from the drawer and lay the table. Even though it's not dark yet, I light a candle. What do I care? This is my party. Dinner for one.

The low point

There I was, in the doorway of my new place, eating cold soup from a plastic container. I'd oiled the wooden floor that day and didn't have any furniture yet. Well, nothing except the landlord's brutally ugly leather sofa, to which for reasons that were beyond me he'd grown attached and would come to pick up in a week's time. Because of the floor, I'd dragged the sofa out on to the roof garden. It was August, and the weather had been sunny for days on end. Carrot soup with ginger, from the refrigerator section of the nearby upmarket foodie supermarket. I was just about to empty the container into a pan to heat it up when I realised that my cooker wasn't yet connected. Damn. I thought about pouring the soup into a glass, but why? Does it feel less pathetic to drink cold soup from a glass than from a plastic container? If so, would that glass be able to save me from the ominous sensation that my life was a complete failure? 'Are you taking care of yourself?' people close to me had asked over these past few months. I was gradually getting scarily thin. How can you eat when you've got a knot the size of a beach ball in your stomach? Since my marriage had fallen

apart I'd been living on smoothies, bananas and soup. Anything I didn't have to chew. As long as I didn't have to cook. I only did the latter on the days I spent with my sons – a sad, monotonous succession of pasta with gloop and rice with gloop. I found it hard to force down even a mouthful.

The soup tasted fine, even cold. Not that this improved my mood, but at least my taste buds noticed. And my mind noticed that my taste buds noticed. I observed that something inside of me was still capable of making observations. And as I sat there in the doorway eating my soup, running circles inside my head, the sky suddenly turned black. Really black. As if Judgement Day were upon us.

A storm of apocalyptic proportions came rolling in over the rooftops of the neighbours at the back, and within a minute it was blowing and raining harder than I'd ever seen it blow and rain during a Dutch summer. Damn – the sofa. I ran out with some plastic sheeting. Pelting rain. Galeforce 3 million. Plastic sheeting fighting back. A four-storey roof garden with no railing. It flashed through my mind that if I fell off now, I would be rid of it all. In the meantime, my body was, luckily, doing its utmost to save both my landlord's sofa and my own skin.

I sat inside, on the freshly oiled floor. I cried. Pretty hard. With mucus and sobs, the whole works. I didn't think I would ever stop, but then all of a sudden I did. I stopped crying and started to laugh. Sounds pretty hysterical, I know, but that's how it was. Then I thought: I'm still alive. Yes, it all sucks big time, and, yes, everything's down to me from here on out, but I'm still alive.

As I drank down the last drops of the cold carrot soup, I resolved that, first thing the next day, I would go out and buy a hose so I could hook up the cooker. And soup bowls. And a few pans. A cutting board. A knife. If I was going to be on my own, I was at least going to take good care of myself. After all, no one else was going to do it for me.

What I've learnt along the way

For more than a year and a half now, I've been on my own part time – my sons live with me half of the week, so that bit doesn't count as alone. The other days I live solo. I put out my own rubbish, replace lightbulbs, top up the boiler, do laundry. And I cook. Do I wish there was someone who would do one of these jobs for me, even if only now and then? Well, sure, sometimes I do.

But more and more often I don't. It took a while, but I've discovered I can live on my own just fine. I have to admit, though, that cooking was the hardest thing of all. For the first nine months my evening meals consisted of supermarket soup, bags of crisps, toasties, fried eggs, mayonnaise, avocado and anchovy sandwiches (which are delicious, by the way!), Indonesian takeaway from the shop around the corner and sometimes just a bowl of oatmeal. Thank god, friends would invite me over from time to time and lovingly feed me healthy home-cooked meals. Then, slowly but surely, as the rawest of my grief over my broken marriage began to recede, my interest in food returned, and with it my enjoyment of cooking. I no longer bought ready-made soups but made them myself. I cooked rice and stir-fried vegetables that I flavoured with ginger, chilli and soy sauce. I sautéed a piece of salmon or fried a steak and ate this with a salad. I cooked spaghetti and made a sport out of getting the sauce ready in exactly the same amount of time as it took to boil the pasta. I ate fewer meals in bed, staring at my laptop, or sprawled on the sofa in front of the television, and more of them sitting at a proper table. I started to stock my new kitchen with a decent supply of basic ingredients so that on busy days, when I came home late, I could still throw together a quick meal. And I started to have fun with it. 'Check me out!' I would say to myself as I sat there all on my lonesome, digging into a delicious plate of risotto. Candles, music, glass of wine. There in the kitchen, during the second half of those first eighteen months following my divorce, I learnt to take care of myself again. I was used to cooking for other people – for my husband, my children, my relatives and my friends – crikey, sometimes I even cooked for the entire street. Cooking was my way of giving pleasure to others, and now I was learning that I deserved that kind of pleasure too. Now I know that cooking for yourself is nothing less than an exercise in loving yourself.

Solo is the new togetherness

More and more people are living solo. Young people, old people, people of all ages. Like me, some of them are divorced; others are widows or widowers, or simply haven't yet found the love of their life. Whatever the reason, more and more people are consciously choosing to live on their own. According to Statistics Netherlands, there are currently more than 3.3 million one-person households. This number is only expected to increase in the decades to come. So, singles are on the rise, and not just in the Netherlands. In Britain the number of people living alone doubled in a generation. More than half of all North Americans are single – that's nearly two and a half times more than in the 1950s. This kind of demographic shift will inevitably have far-reaching economic, political, sociological and cultural consequences.

Don't worry, I won't bore you with the statistics, what I'm concerned with here are the culinary consequences; all those singles who – maybe not every night, but very often – are tucking into their grub on their own. So what does this look like? There's a persistent, clichéd image out there of the single man or woman sitting slouched in front of the television and shovelling down

microwave meals night after night. Or worse yet, eating leftover baked beans straight from the tin by the cold light of the fridge. When I asked around among my single friends, I was relieved to find that things weren't quite so bad. People in single households actually do cook, but almost everyone also admitted that they found it hard to keep their solo meals somewhat interesting, healthy and varied.

Although my little survey may have been totally random and unscientific, the findings are consistent with bona-fide research. On the whole, the meals of people who eat alone are less nutritious than those eaten by people who share their table with others. Singles generally have a more limited diet and eat less fruit, vegetables and fish. These facts are quite disheartening. Statistics also show that singles throw away more food than families. This isn't so strange when you consider that supermarkets still focus mainly on families, with most pre-packaged products intended to serve two to four. So, many of those who eat alone are often obliged to eat the same thing two days in a row. Which is, of course, fine now and then, but does not exactly contribute to the enjoyment of a meal. At the same time, there are hardly any one-person recipes in cookbooks, magazines and newspapers or on cooking blogs and websites.

Cooking for one really does require a different approach from cooking for a family or an entire army and is not simply a matter of quartering a recipe meant for four. Solo cooking requires an approach that is both smarter and simpler. The challenge is to make a proper meal using just a few ingredients (because you want to throw away as little as possible) and not spend too much time doing it (because you don't want to spend an hour in the kitchen every day making something that will take 10 minutes to eat).

Now that solo seems to be the new togetherness, I feel it's high time to finally take the single cook a bit more seriously. Whether you're alone by choice or by chance, whether you eat alone every night or just now and then, I hope this book will help you discover that cooking for yourself can be very satisfying. Perhaps precisely because it's just you. You're essentially your own ideal guest – you know exactly what this person likes to eat.

7 TIPS FOR THE SOLO CHEF

DISCOVER WHAT YOU LIKE TO EAT AND AIM TO PLEASE YOUR OWN PALATE. One of the most wonderful things about cooking for yourself is that you don't have to take anyone else into account. It doesn't matter what you make as long as it sounds good to you.

1

2

EXPERIMENT! See cooking for yourself as a chance to try new things. Even if what you come up with turns out to be inedible, there's no harm done. That's why they deliver pizzas.

STOCK YOUR VERY OWN GOLDEN PANTRY. Cooking for yourself also means you have to do your own shopping, and it's nice if you don't have to leap that hurdle on busy days. On page 23 you'll find a list of food items that are good to always have on hand.

3

4 CUT YOURSELF SOME SLACK. There's nothing wrong with beans from a tin, mayo from a jar, lettuce from a bag or hummus from the refrigerator section of the supermarket. You really don't need to make everything from scratch.

EMBRACE THE ONE-POT MEAL. Cooking for yourself also means you have to do your own washing up … **5**

CHERISH THE EGG. Fried, boiled or scrambled, you can whip up something nourishing in less than 10 minutes. You never have to go hungry if you have eggs in the house. **6**

7 DON'T GO TOO SOLO! Invite friends over for dinner as often as you can. Cooking for yourself is good, and pleasurable, and cool, but I still don't believe that we were meant to eat alone.

YOUR VERY OWN GOLDEN PANTRY

coarse + fine sea salt

black peppercorns

dried herbs + ground spices (in particular thyme, oregano, bay leaves, cumin, coriander, chilli flakes + curry powders)

olive oil + rice or peanut oil

red wine vinegar, white wine vinegar + balsamic vinegar

Dijon mustard

harissa or sambal (Indonesian chilli sauce)

soy sauce

fish sauce

stock cubes and/or stock pots

Thai and/or Indian curry paste

pasta

basmati or jasmine rice + risotto rice

tins or jars of beans, chickpeas and/or lentils

tinned coconut milk

instant couscous and/or bulgur and/or quinoa

instant polenta (if you like polenta – some people hate it)

tins of peeled tomatoes

tinned tuna + anchovies (+ sardines, if you like)

olives in jars or tins

capers, packed in salt or vinegar

nuts (if you freeze them, they'll stay fresh longer)

peanut butter (so you can always make a peanut butter and sambal sandwich)

onions + garlic

eggs

lemons and/or limes

fresh root ginger (you can also cut this into pieces and freeze)

fresh chilli pepper (at least, if you're a chilli-head like me)

butter

yoghurt

Parmesan cheese (can also be frozen, grated or otherwise)

bread

pitta bread and/or tortillas and/or naan (all three can also be used as a base for pizza)

frozen peas and/or spinach

at least 1 portion of meat, chicken or fish

QUICK FIX

Say you come home hungry and tired after a long day at work – cooking yourself anything more than a simple meal would be a challenge, right? To put it mildly. On a night like that all you want to do is kick off your shoes, pour yourself a glass of something and get a plate of food in front of you as quickly as you can. Enter the refrigerated supermarket ready meal. Enter the takeaway.

But the thing with those meals is that they get awfully boring after a while. And do you know why? Because they're prepared by someone who doesn't know you. Someone who doesn't know how hot you like your curry, how salty you like your soup, how velvety you like your mash or how al dente you like your pasta. They're made for the average palate. They haven't been created with unique little you in mind. Which is why a home-cooked meal, no matter how simple, is always more satisfying than an anonymous one. The good news is that it's not that hard to throw something together in 15 minutes – 20 minutes tops. Something that tastes much better and is far more enjoyable …

Cooking for yourself is a chance to figure out what pleases your palate. Or, to paraphrase Nicolas Cage in *Wild at Heart*, see it as a symbol of your individuality and your belief in personal freedom.

A kind of pisto Manchego

Preparation Time
15 minutes

olive oil, for frying
1 small (or ½ large) onion, sliced
  into half rings
½ long red pepper, deseeded
  and sliced into strips
4 slices of Serrano ham or
  chorizo, chopped
½ courgette or 1 baby courgette,
  cut in half lengthways and
  sliced into half moons
10 cherry tomatoes, halved
2 eggs
a few fresh basil or flat-leaf
  parsley leaves (or a pinch of
  dried oregano)
salt and freshly ground pepper,
  to season
bread, to serve

Heat a small splash of olive oil in a frying pan, add the onion and a pinch of salt, and fry for 2 minutes over a high heat until the onion begins to brown. Add the pepper and fry for 2 minutes more. Add the ham or chorizo and fry for another minute. Add the courgette and fry for 2 more minutes. Add the tomatoes and fry for another 2 minutes.

Make two depressions in the vegetable mixture and break in the eggs, then cook for 2–3 minutes until the eggs are set, covering the pan for the last 30 seconds. Sprinkle over a little more salt, if necessary, and in any case with a generous amount of freshly ground pepper and finish with basil or flat-leaf parsley.

Serve immediately with some kind of rustic bread, or just use whatever bread you've got on hand.

Spicy lamb pittas with hummus & garlicky yoghurt

You can make these lamb pittas in the time it would take you to go out and get a takeaway doner kebab – and these are much nicer!

Preparation Time

10 minutes

1 tsp harissa paste

olive oil, for frying

125 g lamb fillet

2 pitta breads

¼–½ garlic clove, crushed or
  pressed

2 tbsp Greek or Turkish yoghurt

a pinch of salt

100 g hummus

a small handful of lettuce leaves

Place a griddle pan over a high heat. Mix the harissa with half a tablespoon of oil and brush this on to the lamb fillet. Set the fillet on the hot griddle and cook for a total of 2–3 minutes, turning regularly – the inside of the meat should still be pink. Place on a cutting board and let it rest.

Meanwhile, cook the pittas in the same pan and stir the garlic and a small pinch of salt into the yoghurt.

Cut the rested meat into thin slices. Slice open the pittas and fill them with hummus, meat, lettuce and a dollop of the garlicky yoghurt.

Miso soup with noodles, shiitake mushrooms, spinach & an egg

Preparation Time

15 minutes

100 g Japanese ramen (or
 other noodles)
1 egg
300 ml vegetable stock (from
 a cube)
100 g shiitake mushrooms, sliced
1 scant tbsp red miso paste
soy sauce, to taste
a small handful of spinach leaves
½ sheet of nori, cut into ribbons
 with scissors or a knife

Prepare the ramen according to the packet instructions.

Soft-boil the egg in a pan of boiling water for 4–5 minutes. Plunge the egg straight into a bowl of cold water to stop it cooking and leave until cool enough to handle. Once cool, peel and cut in half.

Meanwhile, bring the stock to a boil in a small saucepan, add the shiitakes and boil for 1 minute. Put the miso in a bowl, stir in a small splash of the hot stock, then add this to the saucepan. Turn off the heat and stir in soy sauce to taste.

Place the noodles, spinach and the egg halves into a bowl, and pour over the stock and mushrooms. Garnish with nori ribbons to serve.

Ridiculously easy spaghetti caprese

Resist the temptation to add extras like garlic, balsamic vinegar, olives, capers and the like, this dish is all about simplicity and the contrast between hot and cold.

Preparation Time
15 minutes

125 g spaghetti
3 ripe medium-sized vine
  tomatoes
1 small ball of buffalo mozzarella
a small handful of basil leaves
a generous splash of olive oil
salt and freshly ground pepper,
  to season

Cook the spaghetti until just tender in a pan of boiling salted water according to the packet instructions.

Coarsely chop the tomatoes and mozzarella. Tear the basil leaves into small pieces. In a bowl, combine the tomatoes, mozzarella, basil, a generous splash of olive oil, salt and freshly ground pepper.

Drain the spaghetti and mix it into the tomatoes and mozzarella while it's piping hot. And that's it! Eat immediately.

Frittata with red onion, baby kale & goat's cheese

Preparation Time

15 minutes

2 eggs

olive oil, for frying

1 small red onion, sliced into
   half rings

40 g baby leaf kale

few drops of balsamic vinegar

75 g soft goat's cheese

salt and freshly ground pepper,
   to season

Preheat the grill. to high Beat the eggs together with a little freshly ground pepper and a small pinch of salt. Heat a small splash of oil in an ovenproof frying pan over a medium heat, add the onion and a small pinch of salt, and sauté for about 10 minutes. Turn up the heat to high halfway through so that the onion caramelises a little. Then add the baby kale and a few drops of balsamic vinegar, and let the leaves wilt for 30 seconds.

Add the beaten eggs to the pan and make sure the onion and kale are distributed evenly. Dot the goat's cheese over the egg mixture and put the pan under the grill. Leave for a few minutes until the cheese has melted and the omelette is nice and puffy, and cooked through. Serve hot or cold.

Griddled white tuna with cucumber, avocado & ginger salad

Oh, what a wonderful solo supper this is. And what a salad! The spiciness of the chilli pepper, the heat of the ginger and the sour of the lime juice are nothing less than thrilling. The avocado acts as a cool and creamy foil for all of these intense flavours, and if your avocado is very ripe, give the salad a stir and it almost forms a sauce. It might not look all that great, but it tastes divine.

Preparation Time

15 minutes

juice of 1 lime
1 tbsp olive oil
coarse salt, to taste
a small pinch of chilli flakes
1 white (albacore) tuna steak,
    around 150 g
½ cucumber
½ red chilli pepper, sliced into
    thin rings
1½–2 cm root ginger, minced
    or grated
1 ripe avocado, cut in half
    and sliced
soy sauce, to taste

Combine the juice of half the lime, the olive oil, the salt and chilli flakes, and marinate the tuna in this mix for 10 minutes.

Meanwhile, make the salad. Halve the cucumber lengthways and pull a teaspoon down the middle to scoop out and remove the seeds. Cut the cucumber into thin slices and place them in a bowl. Add the chilli rings, ginger and avocado. Sprinkle with the remaining lime juice to taste. The salad should be quite hot and sour. Lastly, add a tiny bit of soy sauce (around a teaspoon) and a pinch of salt.

Heat a griddle pan over a high heat until it's very hot, then add the tuna steak. Griddle for 1 minute on either side until griddle marks appear but the tuna is still pink inside.

Transfer the tuna to a plate and spoon the salad alongside.

Tagliatelle with prawns & smoky whisky–tomato sauce

Preparation Time

15 minutes

100–125 g (fresh) tagliatelle

200 g raw prawns, peeled
  (but with the tail left on) and
  deveined

olive oil, for frying

a splash of whisky

1 small garlic clove, crushed

a pinch of chilli flakes

2 vine tomatoes, finely chopped

a knob of butter

a small handful of flat-leaf parsley
  leaves, finely chopped

coarse salt and freshly ground
  pepper, to season

Cook the tagliatelle in boiling water until just tender, according to the packet instructions.

While the pasta is cooking, sprinkle the prawns with a little salt. Heat a small splash of olive oil in a frying pan and sauté the prawns over a medium–high heat for a few minutes until they're pink and cooked through, then add the whisky to the prawns over the heat. Shake the pan a bit and if you're using a gas hob the contents will ignite on their own. Stand back and let the flames die down, then turn out the prawns on to a plate.

Put the pan back over the heat, add a little more olive oil, if needed, and sauté the garlic and chilli flakes for a minute. Add the tomatoes and cook until they soften and get a little sauce-like, around 3–5 minutes. Add the prawns and the butter, and season with salt and pepper. Add a tiny splash of the pasta cooking water to the sauce, then drain the pasta in a colander.

Add the tagliatelle to the sauce, stir to coat in the sauce, then heat through for another 20–30 seconds. Tip out on to a plate and sprinkle with parsley.

Lemon couscous with salmon & cherry tomatoes

Preparation Time
20 minutes

80 g instant couscous
a small handful of frozen peas
juice and zest of ½ unwaxed
  lemon
a small knob of butter

150 g salmon fillet, with skin
olive oil, for frying
150 g cherry tomatoes (cut any
  big ones in half)
a small handful of flat-leaf parsley
  leaves, coarsely chopped
salt and freshly ground pepper,
  to season

Put the couscous, frozen peas, lemon zest, 1 tablespoon of lemon juice, the butter and a pinch of salt into a bowl. Pour in 125 ml boiling water, cover the bowl with a plate or cling film, and allow to swell for 15 minutes.

Meanwhile, sprinkle the salmon with salt and pepper. Heat a small splash of olive oil in a frying pan and cook the salmon fillet, skin-side down, for a few minutes over a medium–high heat. Turn over and cook for another 1–2 minutes. Make sure you don't overcook the salmon – the middle should still be coral coloured.

Remove the fish from the pan, add the cherry tomatoes to the same pan and cook for 2–3 minutes until soft, shaking the pan occasionally.

When the couscous is ready, fluff it up with a fork then stir in the parsley and taste to see if it needs more lemon or salt. Turn it out on to a plate, place the salmon alongside and spoon over the softened tomatoes.

Salad of butter beans, tinned tuna & shaved fennel

Preparation Time

10 minutes

1 small shallot, sliced into
  thin rings
1 small tin (about 200 g) of butter
  beans
1 small fennel bulb
a small handful of rocket leaves
2–3 fresh mint leaves, finely
  chopped
1 tbsp capers, rinsed, or 1 tbsp
  finely chopped peel from a
  preserved lemon (lemons
  preserved in salt)
juice of ½–1 lemon
a splash of olive oil
1 small tin (120 g) of tuna in
  olive oil
salt and freshly ground pepper,
  to season

Sprinkle the shallot rings with a little salt and let them stand for a bit. Rinse the butter beans under cold running water and drain. Clean the fennel and shave it paper thin on a mandoline, or slice it very thinly with a knife. Squeeze as much liquid as you can out of the shallots.

Mix together the beans, fennel, shallots, rocket, mint and capers or preserved lemon peel, and dress the mixture with lemon juice, a splash of olive oil, salt and freshly ground pepper. Drain the tuna and flake it over the salad in large chunks.

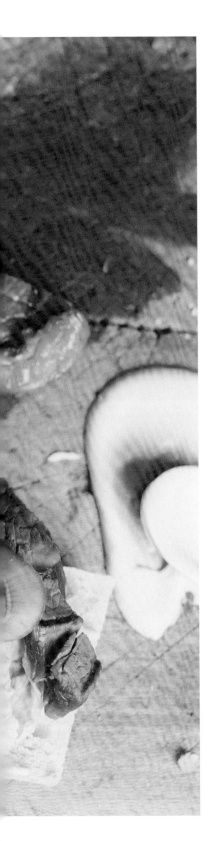

Good old steak sandwich

Preparation Time

15 minutes

1 shallot, sliced into rings
a small splash of red wine
  vinegar
1 entrecôte steak (around 150 g)

¼ baguette or a crusty bread roll
1–2 tsp Dijon mustard
1½–2 tbsp mayonnaise
1 head Little Gem, leaves
  separated
salt and freshly ground pepper,
  to season

Preheat the oven to 200°C/180°C fan/400°F/Gas 6. Put the shallot rings into a small bowl, add the red wine vinegar and let it sit for 10 minutes.

In the meantime, place a griddle pan over a high heat until it's very hot. Rub some salt into both sides of the entrecôte. Fry the meat for 1–1½ minutes on each side. Place it on a cutting board, grind over some pepper and let it rest for a bit.

Warm through the baguette or bread roll in the hot oven (or slice it open and toast in the steak pan). Meanwhile, stir the mustard into the mayo in a little bowl, to taste. Slice the warmed bread in half lengthways, then spread both halves with a generous amount of the mustardy mayo and add some lettuce leaves.

Slice the entrecôte on the diagonal and arrange the slices in the sandwich. Squeeze as much liquid as you can out of the shallot rings and sprinkle them over the meat. Top with the other half of the bread, and dinner is served.

SMART COOKING

One of the things I came up against when I started cooking for myself was that I always ended up with leftovers. I had been used to sharing my table with three hungry men, so I was still figuring out how much I actually ate myself. Does this sound familiar? In my experience you gradually get better at this, but it's still easy to cook too much, especially of things like rice, potatoes and noodles. That's why I've written this chapter, featuring recipes that you can use to turn leftovers from Day 1 into something entirely different on Day 2. Because you don't want to waste food, and you also don't want to eat the same thing day after day. What's more, cooking with leftovers saves time, because rice and potatoes easily need 20 or 25 minutes to prepare. Do it all on Day 1 and that's time you can save on Day 2 so that you're done in 10 or 15 minutes. When cooking solo, it pays to be smart!

Baked sweet potato with olives, feta & chilli

Baking intensifies the sweetness of sweet potatoes and gives the bright orange flesh a kind of fluffiness – light and soft at the same time. Sweet potato is terrific combined with salty olives, creamy feta and hot chilli pepper. It seems a bit wasteful to have the oven blasting for just one or two sweet potatoes, so I often bake a number of them at once. Once baked, you can easily keep them in the fridge for days, or you can use them to make a quick, flavourful soup.

Preparation Time

70-90 minutes

2 very large or 4–5 somewhat
    smaller sweet potatoes
    (about 700 g total)
olive oil, for greasing and
    drizzling
coarse sea salt
50 g creamy feta
a small handful of salty black
    olives, pitted and coarsely
    chopped
½–1 red chilli pepper (with or
    without seeds), sliced into rings
a small handful of fresh coriander
    leaves, coarsely chopped

Preheat the oven to 200°C/180°C fan/400°F/Gas 6. Scrub, rinse and dry the sweet potatoes. Pour a little olive oil on to your palms and rub this over the unpeeled sweet potatoes. Next, rub in some coarse salt. Pierce the sweet potatoes a few times on all sides using a small sharp knife, then wrap them in tin foil and bake for an hour (or a little longer, if necessary) until done. Use half of them immediately and leave the rest to cool (save them for the soup).

Place the sweet potato(es) on a plate and open the foil. Cut in half lengthways, then press on the outside of the halves so that the fluffy flesh bulges out slightly. Crumble the feta over the sweet potato(es), top with the olives, chilli pepper and coriander, and drizzle generously with olive oil.

WHEN COOKING SOLO, IT PAYS TO BE SMART

Sweet potato soup with coconut & fresh coriander

Preparation Time

15 minutes

1 baked sweet potato

rice or peanut oil, for frying

1 tbsp Thai red curry paste

200 ml coconut milk (½ tin, or
   made from a 50 g piece of
   creamed coconut dissolved in
   200 ml hot water)

1 tbsp grated coconut or
   desiccated coconut

zest and juice of 1 lime

Thai fish sauce, to taste

a small handful of fresh coriander
   leaves, coarsely chopped

Cut the baked sweet potato in half, scoop out the flesh and break it into rough pieces. Heat a small splash of oil in a frying pan and fry the curry paste for a minute. Add the coconut milk, 200 ml water and the sweet potato, and bring to the boil. Reduce the heat to low and simmer gently for 5–10 minutes.

Toast the grated or desiccated coconut until light brown in a small, dry frying pan over a medium–high heat, shaking the pan and watching the coconut carefully as it can burn quickly. Remove the pan from the heat, scrub the lime, grate in a little lime zest and mix.

Purée the soup using a hand-held blender and thin with a little more water if you think it's too thick. Try a spoonful, then add lime juice and fish sauce to taste. Pour the soup into a bowl and sprinkle with the lime–coconut topping and the coriander.

Soft polenta with mushrooms & spinach

Take some instant polenta, mushrooms, spinach and an egg, and in 15 minutes you've got a plate of comfort food for one. By cooking twice the amount of polenta and turning half of it out on to a flat plate, this maize porridge will set into a nice flat disc that you can use as a pizza base the following day. If you should happen to end up with some leftover spinach, you can use it to make a salad to eat with your pizza.

Preparation Time

20 minutes

150 g instant polenta
75 g Parmesan cheese
olive oil, for greasing and frying
150 g mushrooms (just one
   kind or a mixture), sliced into
   smaller pieces, if necessary
½ garlic clove, crushed
150 g baby leaf spinach
1 egg
a small knob of butter
salt and freshly ground pepper,
   to season

In a pan, bring 700 ml water to the boil with a pinch of salt. Stir with a whisk as you sprinkle the polenta into the boiling water. Let the mixture cook for 3–5 minutes, or for the time given in the packet instructions. Add extra (boiling) water if necessary – the polenta should be nice and soft. Grate in nearly all of the Parmesan. Taste and season with freshly ground pepper and more salt, if necessary.

When cooked, pour half of the polenta on to a flat plate that you've greased with olive oil, cover with cling film and put in the fridge for tomorrow.

While the polenta cooks, sauté the mushrooms in a small splash of olive oil over a medium–high heat for around 10 minutes. Add the garlic at the end and cook briefly, then sprinkle with salt and pepper. Remove the mushrooms from the pan and add the spinach. Stir-fry the spinach until just wilted. Remove the spinach from the pan and fry an egg (you might need to add another small splash of olive oil).

Stir the butter into the cooked polenta and spoon it into a deep plate. Arrange the mushrooms and spinach on the polenta and top with the fried egg. Season lightly with salt and pepper. Top with the rest of the Parmesan, in slices.

DAY 2

Polenta pizza with blistered cherry tomatoes & anchovies

Preparation Time
15 minutes

olive oil, for frying and drizzling
1 small red onion, sliced into thin
    half rings
a pinch of dried oregano
1 portion polenta, cooled and set
    (see page 54)

7 black olives
3–5 anchovy fillets (from a tin
    or jar)
1 stem of cherry tomatoes, on
    the vine
a few leaves of fresh basil, torn
    into smaller pieces if desired
salt and freshly ground pepper,
    to season

Preheat the grill of your oven to high. Heat a small splash of olive oil in an ovenproof frying pan and fry the onion with a small pinch of salt and the oregano over a medium heat for about 8 minutes. Turn the heat to high and allow the onion to caramelise somewhat, around 5–7 minutes. Remove from the pan. Add another small splash of olive oil to the same frying pan, slide the set polenta into the pan and fry for 2–3 minutes until golden. This is your pizza base.

Arrange the caramelised onion, the olives and the anchovies on top of the polenta, then add the stem of cherry tomatoes. Drizzle with a little olive oil and sprinkle with some salt. Place the pan under the grill for a few minutes until the tomatoes start to blister. Sprinkle the pizza with the basil and a generous grind of pepper and serve.

DAY 1

Mash with baby kale & chorizo

This type of dish is known as a *stamppot* in the Netherlands, which is a kind of comforting winter dish of potatoes mashed with vegetables. Baby kale doesn't need to be cooked – the tender young leaves wilt on their own when you mix them into the hot mashed potatoes. This is ideal for a quick solo mash.

Preparation Time

35 minutes

600 g potatoes

olive oil, for frying

75 g chorizo, chopped into
   small pieces

50–75 ml hot milk

40 g baby kale

red wine vinegar, to taste

salt and freshly ground pepper,
   to season

Scrub the potatoes and cook them in just enough boiling water to cover them in a medium saucepan with a pinch of salt for 20–25 minutes until done. Drain the potatoes, let them sit for a bit to allow the steam to evaporate, then peel them all – the sooner you do this, the easier it will be, so don't let them cool too much. Use half of the potatoes right away for the mash and save the rest for the Patatas a lo pobre (page 63).

Heat a small splash of olive oil in a frying pan and add the chorizo, frying gently until crisp. Mash the potatoes and add enough milk so that you end up with a mixture that is firm yet creamy. Stir in the crispy chorizo (along with the fat from frying it, because that adds flavour!) and the baby kale. Season the mash with a few drops of vinegar and lots of freshly ground pepper.

DAY 2

Patatas a lo pobre

Patatas a lo pobre, or poor man's potatoes, is the Spanish name for fried potatoes with garlic, onions and poached eggs. I first ate this dish in a dark *bodega* in Valencia, and immediately fell in love. If poaching the eggs seems like too much of a chore, you can fry them instead. But whatever you do, make sure the yolk doesn't set; the runny yolk forms a sauce for the potatoes, which is precisely what makes this dish so irresistible.

Preparation Time
15 minutes

olive oil, for frying
1 onion, sliced into rings
2 garlic cloves, thinly sliced
1 portion cold cooked potatoes,
   thickly sliced
2 eggs
a small splash of vinegar
a small handful of flat-leaf parsley
   leaves, coarsely chopped
a pinch of paprika (preferably
   smoked paprika)
salt, to taste

Heat a generous splash of olive oil in a pan (really, don't skimp on this!), add the onion rings and allow them to cook gently over a medium heat until they're caramel coloured, around 15–20 minutes. Add the garlic and cook for a few minutes more. Remove the onions and garlic from the pan and set aside. Now add the potatoes to the pan and fry, still over a medium heat, until they're crunchy and golden brown, about 20–25 minutes.

Meanwhile, poach the eggs in a pan with plenty of boiling water and the vinegar. Or fry them. Add the onion and garlic to the potatoes and sprinkle with parsley, paprika and salt, then give the pan a good shake. Turn the potatoes out on to a plate and place the eggs on top. Sprinkle the eggs with a small pinch of paprika, and you're good to go.

Warm lentil salad with grilled goat's cheese

Preparation Time

30 minutes

250 g Puy lentils (or another
    lentil that holds its shape
    when cooked)

2 tsp red wine vinegar

½ tsp Dijon mustard

½ tsp runny honey, plus extra for
    drizzling (optional)

2–3 tablespoons olive oil, plus
    extra for drizzling

100 g goat's cheese, sliced
    into rounds

a small pinch of dried thyme

12 cherry tomatoes, cut in half

1 spring onion, sliced into rings

a handful of rocket leaves

salt and freshly ground pepper,
    to season

Cook the lentils in a pan with plenty of salted water and a pinch of salt for 20–25 minutes until just tender. Drain the lentils. Use half of them for the salad and set aside the remainder for the soup (see page 66).

Whisk together a dressing using the vinegar, mustard, honey, 2–3 tablespoons olive oil and freshly ground pepper and salt to taste.

Preheat the grill to high. Place the goat's cheese in a baking dish (if you line the dish with a piece of baking parchment you won't have to wash it later) and sprinkle with a little oil and the thyme. Place under the grill until the cheese begins to brown but isn't completely melted, around 2–3 minutes.

Mix together the cooked lentils, cherry tomatoes, spring onion, rocket and dressing, and arrange on a plate. Top with the warm goat's cheese, then drizzle with a little extra honey, if you like.

DAY 2

Spicy lentil soup with yoghurt & rocket

Preparation Time

15 minutes

olive oil, for frying

1 small carrot, diced into
   small cubes

1 celery stalk, sliced crossways
   into little arches

1 garlic clove, crushed

a small pinch of chilli flakes

½ tsp ground cumin

1 portion cooked lentils

salt and freshly ground pepper,
   to season

2–3 tbsp yoghurt, to serve

a small handful of rocket leaves,
   to serve

Heat the olive oil in a pan, add the carrot and celery, and sauté for a few minutes. Add the garlic, chilli flakes and cumin, and fry for another minute. Pour in 400 ml water, add the lentils and bring to the boil, then simmer gently for 10 minutes.

You can either purée the soup with a hand-held blender or leave the lentils and vegetables whole. I often partially purée the soup – in other words, I give the lentils a little whizz but stop before the soup is completely smooth – this way it is velvety but you still have something to sink your teeth into. Taste and season generously with freshly ground pepper and salt.

Pour the soup into a large bowl, add a dollop of yoghurt and scatter over some rocket.

Cod in ginger–tomato sauce with gremolata & rice

Preparation Time

25 minutes

150 g jasmine or basmati rice

olive oil, for frying

2 garlic cloves, crushed

2 cm root ginger, peeled and
  finely chopped

½ red chilli pepper (with or
  without seeds), finely chopped

3 vine tomatoes, coarsely
  chopped

175 g cod fillet

zest of ½ lemon

a small handful of flat-leaf parsley
  leaves, finely chopped

salt and freshly ground pepper,
  to season

Cook the rice according to the packet instructions. Set aside half for the fish and leave the remainder to cool in a covered bowl in the fridge and save it for tomorrow.

Heat a small splash of olive oil in a frying pan and fry three-quarters of the garlic (you'll use the rest for the gremolata), the ginger and the chilli pepper over a medium–high heat for 3 minutes. Add the tomatoes and a small pinch of salt and simmer for 5 minutes, stirring occasionally and breaking up the tomatoes a little bit more with the back of a wooden spoon. Sprinkle the cod with salt and freshly ground pepper and place in the tomato sauce. Reduce the heat to medium and let the fish cook gently in the sauce for about 5 minutes, until just cooked through, flipping it over for the final 2 minutes.

In the meantime, make the gremolata: put the rest of the raw garlic, the lemon zest and the parsley on a chopping board and chop until really fine. Spoon the rice on to a plate and spoon over the fish and tomato sauce. Sprinkle with the gremolata to serve.

YOU NEVER
HAVE TO
GO HUNGRY
IF YOU HAVE
EGGS IN
THE HOUSE

Best-ever fried rice

I once ate this dish at Spice Market, one of Jean-Georges Vongerichten's restaurants in New York. It's simplicity itself, but I've seldom eaten a more delicious plate of rice. His recipe is in the book *Asian Flavors of Jean-Georges*; I've created my own version of it here, but I'm forever grateful to him for the idea. You can have a cucumber salad with this or a leafy green vegetable – steamed or stir-fried and flavoured with a few drops of soy sauce.

Preparation Time

10 minutes

peanut oil, for frying

1 garlic clove, crushed

2 cm root ginger, peeled and
   finely chopped

2 spring onions, sliced into rings

1 portion cold cooked rice

1 egg

1 tsp toasted sesame oil

1 tbsp light soy sauce

salt and freshly ground pepper,
   to season

Heat a small splash of oil in a wok or large frying pan over a high heat. Add the garlic, ginger and a pinch of salt, and stir-fry until crispy and golden brown. Remove from the wok and drain on a piece of kitchen paper. Fry the spring onions gently in the remaining oil, add a small pinch of salt, turn up the heat and add the rice. Stir-fry the rice until it's heated through and piping hot.

Heat a little more oil in a frying pan and fry an egg sunny-side up. Spoon the rice into a deep plate and top with the egg. Drizzle with the sesame oil and soy sauce to taste, and sprinkle with the crispy garlic and ginger.

Chinese egg noodles with steak & oyster sauce

Preparation Time

10 minutes

200 g Chinese egg noodles

125 g steak

½ tsp cornflour

1 tbsp light soy sauce, plus extra
   for serving (optional)

1 tsp toasted sesame oil

rice or peanut oil, for frying

a small handful of sugar
   snap peas

1 tbsp oyster sauce

freshly ground pepper, to season

1 spring onion, sliced into rings
   or matchsticks, to serve

Prepare the noodles according to the packet instructions. Rinse them in a colander under cold running water and drain. Set aside half for tomorrow's noodle salad and use the rest for this dish.

Meanwhile, cut the meat into slices a few millimetres thick. Put the slices into a dish, sprinkle with the cornflour and pour the soy sauce and the sesame oil over the meat. Mix, coat the meat and allow to marinate for 5 minutes. Put a wok over a high heat, wait until it starts to smoke, then pour in a small splash of oil. Stir-fry the meat strips for 1 minute. Add the sugar snaps and stir-fry for 1 minute more. Add the oyster sauce and 1–2 tablespoons of water. Add the drained noodles to the wok and stir-fry for another 30 seconds to heat through. Grind some pepper over the noodles, taste and add more soy sauce, if you like. Sprinkle with the spring onions to serve.

Cold noodle salad with cucumber & sashimi salmon

Preparation Time
10 minutes

1 tbsp light soy sauce
1 tbsp lime or lemon juice
1 tsp toasted sesame oil
1 tsp wasabi paste
a tiny pinch of white sugar

150 g skinless salmon fillet
1 tsp sesame seeds
⅓ cucumber
1 portion cold cooked
   Chinese noodles
1 spring onion, sliced into
   rings or strips
salt, to taste

Whisk together the soy sauce, lime or lemon juice, sesame oil, wasabi, sugar and salt to taste to make a marinade. Cut the salmon into slices of about ½ cm thick (as if you were making sashimi) and marinate these for about 5 minutes.

Toast the sesame seeds quickly in a dry frying pan.

Halve the piece of cucumber lengthways and pull a teaspoon down the middle to scoop out and remove the seeds. Cut into thin slices. Toss together the noodles, cucumber, spring onion and the salmon with the marinade. Sprinkle with the toasted sesame seeds.

NETFLIX DINNER

I know a charming widow who loves to cook. When her husband was
still alive, they would sit at the table for hours, every day. Good food.
Bottle of wine. They'd talk and talk. About their day. About plans for
the future. About life.

She cooks with the same passion now as she did before her husband died.
Just as lovingly, she makes herself something nice to eat, puts her plate
on a tray, adds a glass of wine and plants herself in front of the television.

'Doesn't that feel lonely?' I asked her.

'Not in the least,' she replied. 'In fact, I absolutely love it. Eating in
front of the TV is one of those guilty pleasures I can finally surrender to.'

Looking back, I'm a little embarrassed to say that I was someone who
looked down on eating in front of the television. Eating is something
you do at a table, with all devices turned off and all your attention on the
contents of your plate. It's easy to talk if you're part of a busy family.
Now that I live solo, though, I've pretty much changed my tune. It's a
wonderful thing to lay the table for yourself, complete with candle and
napkin, but there are times when all you want is to snuggle under a
blanket and watch your favourite Netflix series while polishing off a bowl
of food with a spoon. Or a fork – it's entirely up to you. Long live freedom.

Quinotto with fennel, almonds & avocado

This was one of the first things I made for myself after I was on my own. This rather strange combination emerged out of a few things I happened to have on hand. Typical solo food, actually, in that it's something I probably wouldn't make for a guest. But I like it so much that I now eat it fairly often, and every time I do, I hope I'll find the willpower to stop myself from eating the whole bowl. Leftover quinotto (I don't know if this is an actual word, but it seems right here as this is a risotto made from quinoa) also makes a wonderful cold or packed lunch. The hope of having any leftovers, however, is usually in vain.

Preparation Time
25 minutes

olive oil, for frying
1 shallot, sliced into half rings
1 small fennel bulb, cut in half
  and thinly sliced
100 g quinoa
250 ml hot vegetable stock (from
  a cube)
a small handful of almonds, with
  skin on
1 small avocado
juice of ½ lime
a small handful of fresh coriander
  leaves, coarsely chopped
salt and freshly ground pepper,
  to season

Heat the olive oil in a medium saucepan and add the shallot, fennel and a small pinch of salt. Sauté over a medium heat for 5 minutes, then add the quinoa and fry for a further 2 minutes, stirring well. Pour the stock into the pan, bring to the boil, turn down the heat to low, then cover the pan and cook for 15–20 minutes until done.

Toast the almonds in a dry frying pan. Remove the peel from the avocado and cut the flesh into largish chunks – sprinkle them with a little of the lime juice to keep them from turning brown. Remove the pan with the quinoa from the heat and stir in the almonds, avocado and coriander. Taste and season with black pepper, lime juice and, if necessary, a little more salt. Put everything in a bowl, grab a spoon and dig in.

Gnocchi with broad beans, brown butter & crispy sage

Instead of broad beans, you can also make this gnocchi dish with edamame. You know, those green soy beans you can find on the menu at Japanese restaurants or in the freezer cabinet in Asian supermarkets. I always buy shelled edamame, which are sold by the bag.

Preparation Time

15 minutes

40 g butter

5 fresh sage leaves

150 g small broad beans (either fresh ones you've shelled yourself or frozen)

150 g gnocchi

juice of ½ lemon

salt and freshly ground pepper, to season

grated Parmesan cheese, to serve

Bring a pan of water to the boil.

Meanwhile, put the butter and the sage leaves in a small saucepan and place over a low heat. Melt the butter slowly and allow it to brown, around 5–7 minutes – the sage leaves will crisp up on their own. Then turn down the heat as low as it will go.

Add a pinch of salt and the broad beans to the boiling water and boil for 3 minutes. Now add the gnocchi. Cook everything for a further 2–3 minutes until the gnocchi are rising to the surface of the water, then drain in a colander.

Add the gnocchi and beans to the brown butter and sage. Mix gently over a very low heat, then add a squeeze of lemon juice and season with salt and pepper. Turn everything into a shallow bowl and sprinkle generously with Parmesan before tucking in.

Quick aubergine & lamb curry with warm naan

Preparation Time

15 minutes

a pinch of ground cumin
a tiny pinch of ground cinnamon
100 g lamb mince
rice or peanut oil, for frying
1 heaped tbsp tikka masala paste

½ large aubergine, diced
1 naan bread
a generous dollop of full-fat
  yoghurt
a small handful of fresh coriander
  leaves, finely chopped
salt and freshly ground pepper,
  to season

Preheat the oven to 200°C/180°C fan/400°F/Gas 6. Knead the cumin, cinnamon and some salt and pepper to taste into the mince and roll the mixture into 3 small meatballs. Heat a splash of oil in a small sauté pan and fry the meatballs over a medium heat until they're brown all over, around 7–10 minutes. Remove them from the pan on to a plate.

Fry the tikka masala paste for a minute in the remaining fat in the pan and pour in 125 ml water. Add the aubergine dice and bring to the boil. Turn down the heat to medium–high and let it simmer gently for 10 minutes. Return the meatballs to the pan and simmer for another 5 minutes.

Meanwhile, heat the naan in the oven according to the packet instructions. Put the curry into a bowl, top with a dollop of yoghurt and sprinkle with the coriander. You can use the warm naan as an eating utensil by dipping it into the curry, but a spoon is handy, too.

Pasta aglio olio my way

Spaghetti aglio olio e peperoncino **is perhaps the ultimate cook-for-yourself dish. It not only tastes sensational, no matter how often you eat it (and I should know, because I eat it a lot!), but it's also made from basic ingredients that you always have to hand. Another great thing about this dish is that there aren't more than 15 minutes between the moment you think 'I'm hungry' and the moment you're sitting down to a steaming plate of fragrant pasta. And yes, you read it right, this Italian classic contains Thai fish sauce. That isn't as crazy as it sounds when you know that the ancient Romans used garum – the liquid drained from fermented fish – to give their dishes an added savoury kick.**

Preparation Time

15 minutes

100–125 g spaghetti
50 ml olive oil
1–2 garlic cloves, sliced
  paper thin
½ red chilli pepper, finely
  chopped, or a generous pinch
  of chilli flakes
Thai fish sauce, to taste
1 tbsp flat-leaf parsley leaves,
  finely chopped

Cook the spaghetti in a pan of plenty of boiling salted water until just tender, according to the packet instructions.

Meanwhile, heat the olive oil in a saucepan, add the garlic and fry gently for a few minutes without letting it brown. Add the chilli and a tiny splash of fish sauce and let it cook gently for another minute. Drain the spaghetti, but save 1–2 tablespoons of the cooking liquid. Return the spaghetti to the pan together with the reserved cooking liquid, the flavoured oil and the parsley. Place the pan over a low heat and heat everything through for another 30 seconds, stirring constantly. Tip the pasta into a bowl and start eating at once – the hotter it is, the more satisfying it will be.

Green curry with chicken & peas

Of course, there's nothing like fresh spice paste, but you can also make a fragrant green curry in no time using spice paste from a jar. My trick is to finely chop the stems from a bunch of fresh coriander and fry them along with the paste. Instead of peas, you can use broad beans or edamame here.

Preparation Time
20 minutes

100 g jasmine rice
a small handful of fresh coriander
  sprigs
rice or peanut oil, for frying
1 tbsp Thai green curry paste
200 ml coconut milk (½ a tin,
  or made from a 50 g piece of
  creamed coconut dissolved in
  200 ml hot water)
1 lemongrass stalk, bruised
125 g chicken thigh fillet, cut
  into strips
150 g frozen peas
½ tsp white sugar
juice of ½–1 lime
salt, to taste

Cook the rice according to the packet instructions. Pluck the coriander leaves from the stems and set aside, then mince the stems. Place a wok or a large frying pan over a high heat and let it get very hot, then pour in a small splash of oil, add the curry paste and minced coriander stems, and fry for 1–2 minutes. Pour in the coconut milk and bring it to the boil. Add the lemongrass and chicken, and allow to cook gently for 5 minutes. Add the peas and cook for a few minutes more.

Fish out the lemongrass and discard. Taste and season the curry with sugar, salt and lime juice. There should be a nice balance of sweet, salty, sour and hot.

Spoon the rice into a bowl, spoon over the curry and sprinkle with the reserved coriander leaves.

Warm salad of new potatoes & peppered mackerel

Preparation Time

15 minutes

200 g baby potatoes (unpeeled),
  scrubbed

150 g peppered smoked
  mackerel

½ box of garden cress

1 tbsp capers

juice of ½ lemon

olive oil

salt and freshly ground pepper,
  to season

Put the potatoes in a large pan, cover with water and bring to the boil. Add salt to taste and cook until done, around 15–20 minutes. Drain.

Break the mackerel into flakes and remove any bones. Cut the cooked potatoes in half and put them in a bowl along with the mackerel, cress and capers. Add the lemon juice, olive oil, salt and pepper to taste, and toss everything together.

Spaghetti with cherry tomatoes, nutmeg & ricotta

For this dish I borrowed just a teeny little bit from a recipe in one of the books from the renowned London restaurant The River Café. It turns out that freshly grated nutmeg is a surprisingly wonderful addition to tomato sauce.

Preparation Time

15 minutes

125 g spaghetti
olive oil, for frying
1 garlic clove, thinly sliced
200 g cherry tomatoes, cut in half
freshly grated nutmeg (not too
    much), to taste
a small handful of basil leaves
salt and freshly ground pepper,
    to season
2 heaped tbsp ricotta, to serve
grated Parmesan cheese,
    to serve

Cook the spaghetti in a pan of boiling salted water until just tender, according to the packet instructions.

Heat a small splash of olive oil in a frying pan and fry the garlic for 2 minutes until it's cooked but not brown. Turn up the heat and add the tomatoes. Sprinkle with a little salt and freshly ground pepper, and cook the tomatoes for about 2 minutes, occasionally giving the pan a good shake. Add grated nutmeg to taste and let it cook for another minute.

Pour a tiny splash of pasta water into the sauce and then tip the pasta into a colander. Allow to drain and add to the sauce. Then add the basil and heat for another 30 seconds until everything is hot. Turn into a bowl, spoon on the ricotta and sprinkle with Parmesan to serve.

Orecchiette with Tenderstem broccoli, anchovies & fennel seed

For this pasta dish, you can also use regular broccoli or green asparagus instead of Tenderstem broccoli.

Preparation Time

15 minutes

125 g orecchiette, or another
 short pasta
olive oil, for frying
1 garlic clove, crushed
3–4 anchovy fillets (from a tin
 or jar), drained and finely
 chopped
a small pinch of chilli flakes
a pinch of fennel seeds
100 g Tenderstem broccoli,
 roughly chopped
a few drops of red wine vinegar
salt and freshly ground pepper,
 to season
grated pecorino or Parmesan
 cheese, to serve (optional)

Cook the pasta in a pan of boiling salted water until just tender, according to the packet instructions. Drain, saving 2 tablespoons of the cooking water.

Heat a splash of olive oil in a sauté pan and gently fry the garlic, anchovies, chilli flakes and fennel seeds. Add the broccoli pieces and fry for 1 minute more. Next add the reserved 2 tablespoons of cooking water, cover the pan, turn the heat down to low and cook for 1–2 minutes until the broccoli is tender.

Season to taste with salt and pepper and a few drops of vinegar. Add the drained orecchiette and heat through for another 30 seconds while you gently shake the pan to combine. Put the pasta into a bowl and sprinkle with cheese, if desired.

COOKING FOR YOURSELF IS AN EXERCISE IN LOVING YOURSELF

Courgette soup with tarragon

Some nights all you need is a (big!) bowl of soup. This one is creamy and mild, and the raw courgette you add right at the end gives the soup a pleasant bite. Should you decide to eat something with it, I find that somehow this soup goes perfectly with a cream cheese and smoked salmon bagel.

Preparation Time
20 minutes

olive oil, for frying
1 shallot, finely chopped
1 potato, peeled and diced
1 courgette, chopped
a small splash of dry white
   vermouth (if you happen to
   have it to hand)
250 ml stock (vegetable,
   chicken or beef, from a stock
   cube or pot)
leaves from 1 sprig of tarragon
salt and freshly ground pepper,
   to season
a small splash of whipping cream

Heat a small splash of oil in a large pan and gently fry the shallot and potato for 5 minutes. Reserve a small piece of the courgette, then add the rest to the pan and fry just a little bit longer. Deglaze the pan with the vermouth, if you're using it. Pour in the stock, add the tarragon leaves, bring everything to the boil, turn the heat to low and let it cook for 10–15 minutes, until the potato and courgette are tender.

Finely dice the reserved courgette. Purée the soup with a hand-held blender until smooth, then add salt and freshly ground pepper to taste. Add a little more stock or water if it's too thick. Pour the soup into a bowl, swirl in the cream and garnish with the diced raw courgette.

Bowl of rice with Chinesey vegetables

Preparation Time

20 minutes

100 g jasmine or basmati rice

rice or peanut oil, for frying

1 shallot, finely chopped

1½–2 cm root ginger, peeled and
thinly sliced into matchsticks

½ red chilli pepper (with or
without seeds), sliced into rings

1 small head of broccoli, divided
into florets

150 g oyster mushrooms, torn
in half

1 tbsp Shaoxing rice wine or
dry sherry

1–2 tbsp light soy sauce

a small handful of cashew nuts

salt, to taste

Cook the rice according to the packet instructions.

Place a wok over a high heat and wait until it starts to smoke.
Pour in a small splash of oil and stir-fry the shallot, ginger
and chilli pepper for 30 seconds. Add the broccoli florets and
stir-fry for 1 minute. Add a small splash of water and keep
stirring until the broccoli is nearly tender and the water has
evaporated, around 5–7 minutes. Add the oyster mushrooms
and stir-fry another 1 minute. Pour the Shaoxing or sherry and
the soy sauce into the wok and add a pinch of salt. Spoon the
cooked rice into a bowl, top with the vegetables and sprinkle
with the cashews.

FREEZE YOUR FAVOURITES

His belly is filled with a totally systemless collection of containers, bags, packages, bowls, tubs, boxes, foil wrappers, ice crystals, breadcrumbs and orphaned peas. He's often only willing to open his mouth if I threaten to use violence, yet I love him all the same. Call me a squirrel, but a jam-packed freezer can make me a very happy woman. It's so comforting to know that all of those packages with lovely home-cooked meals are there waiting for me, ready to be thawed out and heated up when I don't have the time or don't feel like cooking. You don't have to cook every single day – it's ok to do things the easy way once in a while.

The one thing I'd still like to master is to keep him neat and tidy, with matching white freezer containers bearing labels with contents and date. A frosty, frozen biotope, where I can go straight to what I'm looking for instead of freezing my fingers digging for it (dream on, girl!). But, be that as it may, if you're living solo, your freezer is your best friend. So I present to you this chapter, with recipes for soups, sauces, stews and even one for nasi goreng, a dish that freezes surprisingly well. Make it easy on yourself: freeze your favourites.

Chilli con everything

Preparation Time

1 ¾ hours

Makes 4 Portions

For the chilli

olive oil, for frying

350 g beef mince

1 onion, finely chopped

2 garlic cloves, crushed

1–2 red chilli peppers (with or
  without seeds), finely chopped

2 tsp ground cumin

1½ tsp dried oregano

1 tsp cayenne pepper

2 tbsp whisky (optional)

1 x 400 g tin of chopped
  tomatoes

250 ml beef stock (from a cube)

2 x 400 g tins of beans, drained
  and rinsed (haricot, black,
  kidney or a mixture)

15 g dark chocolate (70%
  cocoa solids), finely chopped
  (optional)

salt and freshly ground pepper,
  to season

Toppings for your chilli

finely chopped red onion

diced avocado

roughly chopped fresh coriander

soured cream

grated cheese

tortilla chips

This spicy chilli is flavourful enough to eat plain, but there's nothing stopping you jazzing it up with everything under the sun. Although the whisky in the recipe gives it just that little bit more depth, it's not essential. The same applies to the chocolate. I love it in chilli, but if you don't, just leave it out. You can serve this with bread, if you like, or rice, or even with a nice big pile of tortilla chips.

Heat the olive oil in a heavy casserole and brown the mince well, breaking it up as it cooks, around 7–10 minutes, on a medium–high heat. Remove from the pan. Fry the onion in the fat left in the pan, another 5 minutes. Add the garlic and chillies, and fry a bit longer, then return the mince to the pan. Now add the cumin, oregano, cayenne pepper and a generous pinch of salt, and fry for another 2 minutes. If you're using it, add the whisky to the pan and give the meat mixture another stir. Add the tomatoes and stock, bring to the boil, turn the heat down to low and cover, placing the lid slightly askew. Simmer the chilli for 1 hour.

Add the beans and simmer for another 15 minutes. If you're using it, stir in the chocolate at the end. Taste and add more salt if necessary, or make it even hotter with extra cayenne pepper. You now have 4 portions of chilli.

To eat at once: Ladle into a bowl and sprinkle with toppings.

To freeze: Divide among freezer containers, seal and freeze.

To reheat: Take a container out of the freezer in the morning and put it in the fridge. The chilli will be (nearly) thawed in the evening. Heat in a saucepan, or thaw and heat the chilli in the microwave.

All-round chicken soup

Chicken soup. As soon as there's anything wrong with me, whether it's a runny nose or a broken heart, this is what I crave. And I want someone else to make it for me! But – too bad, so sad – that's not on the cards if you live on your own. Which is why I always have a supply of chicken soup in the freezer.

Preparation Time

3–4 hours

Makes 4 Portions

1 chicken, around 1.25 kg

75 g fresh root ginger (unpeeled), sliced

5 kaffir lime leaves

2 lemongrass stalks, bruised

1 tsp black peppercorns

1 tsp salt

Put the chicken in a large saucepan along with the ginger, kaffir lime leaves, lemongrass, peppercorns and salt. Pour in 1¾ litres of cold water and let it slowly come to the boil. Use a skimmer or slotted spoon to remove the foam from the surface and discard. Place a lid on the pan at a slight angle and leave the stock to simmer very gently for 3–4 hours, turning the chicken every now and then for even cooking.

Pour the stock through a colander or strainer to strain out the chicken and herbs. Remove the skin from the chicken and discard; pull the meat off the bones and separate into shreds. You now have around 1½ litres of stock and a pile of chicken shreds.

To eat at once: Bring a portion of the stock to the boil together with a portion of the meat. If you like, you can put noodles or rice and other extras into a bowl and pour in the soup.

To freeze: You can put the shredded chicken back into the stock and divide this among the freezer containers and freeze them this way. However, I like to freeze the stock and meat separately. This way, one time you can make soup with the stock and the chicken shreds, and another time you can just thaw the stock and add in some shrimp, for example, or a hard-boiled egg.

To reheat: Thaw one portion of the stock and one portion of the chicken in the fridge, then heat them together in a saucepan. Make sure you let the stock come to the boil at least briefly.

Or thaw the frozen stock in the microwave, then pour it into a pan and bring to the boil briefly. You can thaw the chicken in the microwave, too, but it also thaws really quickly if you add the frozen meat to the gently simmering stock.

THE FOLLOWING ITEMS CAN BE ADDED TO THE SOUP OR USED AS A GARNISH
- Thin glass or rice noodles, Chinese egg noodles, vermicelli, cooked rice, cubes of cooked potato.
- Sliced spring onions, fresh small red chilli peppers (bird's-eye chillies), finely chopped fresh coriander or celery leaves, bean sprouts, packaged crispy fried onions.
- Thai fish sauce, Japanese soy sauce, ketjap manis (Indonesian sweet soy sauce), sambal (Indonesian chilli sauce), lime or lemon juice.
- Shredded chicken from the stock, a hard-boiled egg, a thin omelette sliced into ribbons, or shrimp.

Comforting little casseroles

Tender, sweet and well-spiced stewed meat topped with cheese-encrusted creamy mashed potatoes... need I say more? True, they do take time, but when you're done you'll have a wealth of comfort food to squirrel away for later.

Preparation Time
about 2 ½ hours

Makes 4 Portions
For the stewed beef:
600 g stewing beef,
    cut into cubes
50 g butter
olive oil, for frying
3 onions, finely chopped
1 bottle of dark beer
2 tbsp white wine vinegar
1 tbsp wholegrain mustard
½ tsp ground ginger
1 bay leaf
1 thick slice of ginger loaf
    (about 50 g)
salt and freshly ground pepper,
    to season

For the mashed potatoes:
1 ¼ kg floury potatoes, peeled
    and cut into large chunks
150–200 ml hot milk
50 g butter
2 egg yolks
125 g grated mature
    Cheddar cheese
freshly grated nutmeg

Sprinkle the meat with salt and freshly ground pepper, and let it rest for 5 minutes. Heat the butter and a small splash of oil in a heavy-based pan and brown the meat, in batches, over a high heat on all sides, around 3–5 minutes in total. Remove from the pan and set aside.

Fry the onions in the fat in which you fried the meat until they're starting to get quite brown, around 10 minutes. Pour in the beer and the vinegar, and add the mustard, ground ginger and bay leaf. Crumble in the gingerbread and return the meat to the pan. Bring everything to the boil, cover with a lid and turn the heat down as low as you can. Stew the meat for around 2 hours, stirring occasionally, until it's very tender. You might need either to add a little more liquid, or boil down the cooking liquid at the end.

Meanwhile, make the mashed potatoes. Place the potatoes in a large saucepan and add just enough water to cover. Lightly salt. Bring to the boil, then partially cover the pan and simmer for around 20–25 minutes, until tender. Drain and mash together with the hot milk and butter until smooth. Mix in the egg yolks and half of the grated cheese, then season with salt, pepper and nutmeg to taste.

Taste the stewed meat and add salt and pepper if necessary. Divide among 4 small ovenproof casserole dishes and top with a layer of mashed potato. Sprinkle with the rest of the grated cheese.

To eat at once: Place a casserole in an oven preheated to 200°C/180°C fan/400°F/Gas 6until the cheese has melted, around 10 minutes. If you like, you can put it under the grill for the last few minutes of baking to give you a crisp brown crust.

To freeze: Wrap the casseroles, dish and all, in freezerproof cling film or put in a freezer bag, and freeze.

To reheat: Thaw (for example, you can take one out of the freezer in the morning and put it in the fridge – it will then be thawed when you come home in the evening). Unwrap and heat for 20–25 minutes in a 200°C/180°C fan/400°F/Gas 6 oven. You can also heat the casseroles straight from the freezer if necessary – this will take 45–60 minutes in a 200°C/180°C fan/400°F/Gas 6 oven.

Roasted squash & carrot soup

Roasting the squash, carrots and onion in the oven first makes them wonderfully sweet, then you just turn them into soup. Freeze three of the portions and eat one portion right away with one of the extras, if you like.

Preparation Time

about 1¼ hours

Makes 4 Portions

500 g carrots, peeled and cut
  into large chunks
1 small butternut squash,
  scrubbed (if organic) or
  peeled (if not), chopped
  into large chunks
2 onions, quartered
olive oil, for roasting
1 litre vegetable stock (from
  a cube)
1 sprig of rosemary
salt and freshly ground pepper,
  to season

Preheat the oven to 200°C/180°C fan/400°F/Gas 6. Toss the carrots, squash and onion chunks with a splash of oil and a pinch of salt, and spread on a baking sheet covered with baking parchment. Roast the vegetables in the oven for around 45 minutes until they're more or less soft.

Tip the roasted vegetables into a saucepan and add the stock and the rosemary sprig. Bring everything to the boil, turn down the heat to low and let the soup cook for another 15 minutes. Remove the rosemary and purée the soup with a hand-held blender. This soup is quite thick. If you like your soup thinner, you can add a little more water or stock.

Taste and season the soup with salt and a generous amount of freshly ground pepper. You now have 4 portions of soup.

To eat at once: You can add some extras, if you like (see opposite).

To freeze: Divide the soup among freezer containers, seal and freeze.

To reheat: Take a container out of the freezer in the morning and put it in the fridge. The soup will be (nearly) thawed by evening. Heat in a saucepan, or thaw and heat the soup in the microwave.

IN OR ALONG WITH THE SOUP

- Garnish with a drizzle of olive oil and Parmesan flakes.
- Garnish with a dollop of crème fraîche and some snipped chives.
- Fry cubes of stale bread in olive oil together with a garlic clove and some finely chopped rosemary and float them in the soup.
- Place a small handful of rocket leaves tossed with olive oil, salt and lots of freshly ground pepper on top of the soup.
- Make the soup a little spicier with a few drops of Tabasco or rings of chilli pepper and also add a squeeze of lemon or lime juice.
- Make crostini by toasting slices of French bread or ciabatta and topping them with Gorgonzola (or try goat's cheese) and putting them under the grill briefly.

Pasta sauce with fresh sausage & fennel seed

Sausage meat has a much higher fat content than mince and has more flavour for this reason alone. Even if, like I always do, you throw away some of the fat after frying, you will end up with a much richer sauce.

Preparation Time
about 1 hour

Makes 4 Portions
olive oil, for frying

1 large onion, finely chopped

2 celery stalks, sliced crossways
    into arches

2 garlic cloves, crushed

1 tsp fennel seeds

½ tsp chilli flakes

500 g fresh sausages

2 x 400 g tins of chopped
    tomatoes

250 ml red wine

salt and freshly ground pepper,
    to season

Heat a small splash of oil in a large frying pan over a medium heat, and fry the onion and celery together with a pinch of salt. After about 5 minutes, add the garlic, fennel seeds and chilli flakes, and cook for another 2 minutes.

Meanwhile, slice open the sausages lengthways and remove the meat from the casings. Crumble the meat into the pan with the vegetables and spices, add another splash of olive oil then let it brown, breaking it up with the back of a wooden spoon, around 10 minutes. Add the undrained chopped tomatoes and wine, and bring to the boil. Reduce the heat to low and let it cook gently for 45 minutes–1 hour. Taste and season with salt and pepper. You now have 4 portions of pasta sauce.

To eat at once: Cook some pasta until just tender. Drain, reserving 2 tablespoons of the cooking liquid. Return the pasta to the pan, add the reserved cooking liquid and a portion of the pasta sauce, and stir as you heat through for another 30 seconds.

To freeze: Divide among freezer containers, seal and freeze.

To reheat: Take one of the containers out of the freezer in the morning and put it in the fridge. The sauce will be thawed by evening. Heat the sauce in a saucepan, or thaw and heat the sauce in the microwave.

Pork loin stewed with red wine & bay leaves

Preparation Time

1 ¾ hours

Makes 4 Portions

600 g pork loin, cut into cubes

olive oil, for frying

1 large onion, finely chopped

2 celery stalks, chopped into
   small cubes

3 garlic cloves, crushed

2 bay leaves

a large sprig of rosemary

400 ml red wine

1 x 400 g tin of chopped
   tomatoes

salt and freshly ground pepper,
   to season

Sprinkle the meat with salt and freshly ground pepper. Heat a splash of olive oil in a heavy casserole and brown the meat on all sides, in batches, around 5 minutes per batch over a high heat. Remove the pork from the casserole. Reduce the heat to medium–high then add the onion and celery, and fry for 8 minutes, stirring well. Add the garlic, bay leaves and rosemary sprig, and cook for another 2 minutes. Now pour in the red wine and let it bubble for 5 minutes.

Turn down the heat to low, add the pork back to the dish and let it simmer for 15 minutes. Add the undrained chopped tomatoes and ½ a teaspoon of salt. Cover the pan with a lid and let it simmer for another hour (or a little longer) on a very low heat until the meat is tender. You now have 4 portions of stew.

To eat at once: Make some mashed potatoes or rice to serve with it, or cook some oven chips or get some from the chippy.

To freeze: Divide the stew among freezer containers, seal and freeze.

To reheat: Take a container out of the freezer in the morning and put it in the fridge. The stew will be (nearly) thawed in the evening. Heat in a saucepan, or thaw and heat the stew in the microwave.

Marcella's sugo

This sugo *al pomodoro* is based on a famous recipe by Italian writer Marcella Hazan. The sauce is irresistible in its simplicity. Where Hazan uses butter, I use olive oil instead. That felt like sacrilege at first, but I like it better. Marcella has you throw away the stewed onion, which is a real shame – I always munch it down with a drizzle of olive oil, salt and freshly ground pepper.

Preparation Time
45 minutes

Makes 4 Portions
75 ml olive oil
1 kg ripe tomatoes, skins
   removed (see page 116) and
   cut into large chunks (or 2 x
   400 g tins of peeled tomatoes)
1 onion, cut in half
salt, to season

Put the olive oil, tomatoes, onion and a pinch of salt into a medium saucepan and simmer gently for 45 minutes, uncovered, until the fat is floating above the tomatoes. Stir occasionally, and crush any large tomato chunks with a wooden spoon. Taste and add a little more salt if necessary. Remove the onion chunks. You now have 4 portions of sauce.

To eat at once: Add one of the extras to the sauce, if you like (see opposite), and mix it into pasta (cooked until just tender), or try one of the other suggestions.

To freeze: Divide the sugo among freezer containers, seal and freeze.

To reheat: Take a container out of the freezer in the morning and put it in the fridge. The sauce will be (nearly) thawed in the evening. Heat in a saucepan, or thaw and heat the sauce in the microwave.

HERE ARE SOME SUGGESTIONS OF HOW TO USE THIS VERSATILE SAUCE

AS PASTA SAUCE

- As is, with grated Parmesan and maybe some fresh basil.
- With tuna (from a tin) and capers mixed in.
- With sliced black olives, capers, a pinch of chilli flakes and flat-leaf parsley.
- With slivers of bacon or pancetta that you've fried until crisp.
- With mince that you've fried first.

AS PIZZA SAUCE

- Spread the sauce on a ready-made pizza base and add your favourite toppings.

AS A SAUCE FOR LAMB, CHICKEN OR FISH

- Fry an extra garlic clove and a pinch of ground cumin in some olive oil and add the sauce.

FOR COOKING FISH

- Dissolve a few finely chopped anchovy fillets in a little olive oil over a very low heat and add the sauce. Place a piece of white fish fillet in the sauce and simmer gently until the fish is cooked through.

AS A QUICK SOUP

- Thin a portion of sauce with stock (from a jar or cube). Bring to the boil briefly and purée with a hand-held blender, if you like. Garnish with fresh basil and a drizzle of olive oil.

Pesto at your fingertips

Making pesto is a cinch if you have a food processor, but you do have to have a lot of fresh basil on hand. It can be quite handy, then, to make a good supply of pesto in one go. Pesto freezes well and thaws very quickly, too, which means it really is possible to have a pasta dish on the table in less than 10 minutes.

Preparation Time

10 minutes

Makes 4 Portions

1 large garlic clove

40 g almonds, hazelnuts or other
   nuts (blanched)

½ tsp coarse sea salt

40 g basil leaves

60 g grated Parmesan cheese

150 ml olive oil

salt and freshly ground pepper,
   to season

Place the garlic, nuts and a pinch of salt in the bowl of the food processor, and pulse until finely ground. Add the basil and Parmesan, and pulse a few more times. Now, with the machine running, gradually add the olive oil until the mixture is nicely emulsified. Taste and season the pesto with salt and freshly ground black pepper.

Or, if you don't own a food processor, pound and grind the garlic, nuts and basil along with a pinch of salt in a mortar, add the Parmesan, then gradually add the olive oil.

To eat at once: Mix a portion of the pesto into pasta that has been cooked until just tender. Add a small splash of the pasta cooking water to make it creamier. You can also cook a handful of green beans along with the pasta – they combine very well with pasta pesto, and you'll be getting some vegetables too.

To freeze: Divide among freezer containers, seal and freeze.

To reheat: Take a container out of the freezer in the morning and put it in the fridge. The pesto will be thawed by evening, or thaw a portion of pesto by floating the container in a bowl of hot water. At a pinch, you can also thaw the pesto in the microwave, but do this in short bursts because you definitely don't want to overheat it.

Ratatouille

Some things just aren't meant to be made in small quantities. Like ratatouille. Yes, in theory, you could stew together half an onion, one garlic clove, half a courgette, half an aubergine and one tomato for an hour and a half, but it wouldn't really make any sense when you could just as easily make an entire pan. And, what's more, in some wonderful way ratatouille's flavour only seems to get better over time, whether you store it in the fridge (it easily keeps for 4 days or so) or in the freezer. So here you have a recipe for a panful of ratatouille.

Preparation Time

about 2 hours

Makes 4 Portions

150 ml olive oil

2 large white onions, sliced into
   half rings

4 garlic cloves, sliced

2 aubergines, cut in half
   lengthways, then into thick
   half moons

2 long sweet red peppers,
   deseeded and sliced into rings

2 courgettes, cut in half
   lengthways and then into thick
   half moons

4 sprigs of thyme

2 bay leaves

500 g fresh tomatoes

salt and freshly ground pepper,
   to season

Heat the olive oil in a casserole and add the onions along with a pinch of salt. Fry over a medium heat for 20 minutes, but don't allow them to brown. Turn up the heat a little, add the garlic and cook for a further 2 minutes. Add the aubergines and stir as you cook for 5 minutes more. Then add the sweet peppers, and after 4 minutes add the courgette, thyme and bay leaves and a touch more oil, if needed. Stir well, cover the pan, turn down the heat to low and simmer for 45 minutes.

Remove the skin from the tomatoes by scoring a cross into their rounded ends and plunging them into a bowl of boiling water for 30–40 seconds. Remove from the water and pull off the skin, then cut the tomatoes into large chunks. Add the chunks to the pan and bring everything to the boil again. Cover the pan, turn the heat to low and let it simmer for another 30 minutes. The vegetables should be completely soft but have still retained (some of) their shape.

The vegetables might also be swimming in liquid. If that's the case, remove them from the pan with a skimmer or slotted spoon and place them in a dish. Turn the heat under the pan to high and reduce the liquid to a thick syrup.

Return the vegetables to the pan and season to taste. You now have 4 portions of ratatouille.

To eat at once: Let the ratatouille cool slightly before you eat it. That might sound strange, but it tastes better lukewarm than it does piping hot. For options, see below.

To freeze: Divide the ratatouille among freezer containers, seal and freeze.

To reheat: Take a container out of the freezer in the morning and put it in the fridge. The ratatouille will be (nearly) thawed in the evening. Eat it at room temperature, or heat in a saucepan, or thaw and heat the ratatouille in the microwave.

EVERY TIME YOU THAW A PORTION, YOU CAN EAT YOUR RATATOUILLE IN A DIFFERENT WAY
- With lamb chops that you've marinated briefly with a little olive oil, garlic and rosemary, and then cooked on a griddle pan.
- With a piece of fried fish.
- On toast, with crumbled goat's cheese – then put under the grill for a bit, yum!
- And you can also give this a try: heat the ratatouille in a saucepan, make 1–2 holes in the mixture and break in 1–2 eggs. You can either let the eggs cook until the whites are firm and the yolks are still a little runny, or stir with a fork so that you end up with what resembles messy scrambled eggs.

Surinamese masala chicken

It's not essential, but if you like you can use a Madame Jeanette chilli pepper in this dish. I always find it gives it that little bit of an extra Surinamese *je ne sais quoi*. But watch out – those things are hot as blazes, so don't cut it up into little pieces, add the pepper whole.

Preparation Time

1¼ hours

Makes 4 Portions

8 chicken drumsticks

rice or peanut oil, for frying

1 onion, finely chopped

3 garlic cloves, crushed

2 tbsp curry powder

2 tbsp dark soy sauce, plus extra to taste

1 Madame Jeanette chilli pepper or Scotch Bonnet chilli pepper (optional)

a small handful of celery leaves

salt and freshly ground pepper, to season

Sprinkle the drumsticks with salt. Heat the oil in a large heavy-based casserole and brown the chicken, in batches, on all sides over a high heat for around 5–7 minutes. Remove from the pan. Fry the onion for a 5–7 minutes in the fat from the chicken. Add the garlic and curry powder and fry for another 2–3 minutes, stirring constantly. Add 250 ml water and the dark soy sauce and return the chicken to the pan. If you're using it, tuck the (whole, uncut!) chilli in amongst the drumsticks. Bring to the boil, turn down the heat to low, cover the pan, and simmer for around an hour.

Taste and season with a little more dark soy sauce, salt and pepper, if necessary. Sprinkle with the celery leaves to serve (although you needn't add these if you're planning to freeze your dish as the leaves will wilt in the freezer).

To eat at once: Eat with roti or rice.

To freeze: Divide the chicken and sauce among freezer containers, seal and freeze.

To reheat: Take a container out of the freezer in the morning and put it in the fridge. The chicken will be (nearly) thawed in the evening. Heat in a saucepan, or thaw and heat the chicken in the microwave.

Basic nasi goreng (Indonesian fried rice)

Preparation Time

20 minutes

Makes 4 Portions

For the spice paste (bumbu)

3–4 shallots or 1 large onion,
  coarsely chopped

3 garlic cloves

3–4 cm root ginger, peeled and
  finely chopped

1–2 red chilli peppers (seeds
  and all), coarsely chopped

1 tsp (Indonesian) shrimp paste
  (trassi)

2 tsp curry powder

1 tsp ground coriander

1 tsp ground cumin

a pinch of salt

For the rice

300 g pork tenderloin, cut
  into strips

peanut oil, for frying

100 g smoked bacon, cut
  into strips

300 g rice (uncooked weight),
  cooked and cooled

1 leek, sliced into thin rings

200 g sweetheart or white
  cabbage, sliced into thin strips

around 2 tbsp dark soy sauce

salt and freshly ground pepper,
  to season

Having a decent takeaway restaurant around the corner, with decent hours (read: open until late) is a blessing for anyone living on their own. There is an excellent Indonesian one just near me, and I stop in regularly to get something to go. Although this is nice, and easy, to do, it's also relatively expensive. With just a little effort, you can make yourself a few portions of nasi goreng and then, whenever you like, you can pull one out of the freezer, heat it up and garnish it with a few fresh ingredients. One thing: nasi goreng is best made using cold rice, so make sure you cook it well ahead of time.

To make the spice paste, purée all of the ingredients, plus a pinch of salt, in the food processor, or grind them in a mortar.

Sprinkle the pork strips with salt and freshly ground pepper. Heat 1 tablespoon of oil in a wok or large frying pan and fry the bacon strips over a medium–high heat until crisp, around 5–7 minutes. Remove from the wok. Add a splash of oil and fry the pork for 5–8 minutes until done. Remove from the pan.

Now fry the spice paste for 2–3 minutes in the fat left over from frying the meat (or add a tablespoon of oil if necessary). Add the cold rice and toss with two spatulas until the rice starts to get a little crunchy (3–4 minutes). Add the leek and fry a bit more (2–3 minutes), then add the cabbage and fry for a further 2 minutes. Return the bacon and pork to the wok with the soy sauce and toss. You now have 4 portions of basic nasi goreng.

To eat at once: Add one of the extras (see below) and enjoy your meal!

To freeze: Divide the nasi goreng among freezer containers, seal and freeze. (The containers from your takeaway meals are often ideal for this purpose.)

To reheat: Take a container out of the freezer in the morning and put it in the fridge. The rice will be (nearly) thawed in the evening. Reheat thoroughly in a frying pan and add one of the extras (see below), if you like.

EXTRAS TO HAVE WITH NASI GORENG

- Eat it with a fried egg or thin omelette (whisk an egg together with ½ a tablespoon of water, ½ a tablespoon of light soy sauce and some freshly ground pepper).
- When you're reheating the nasi goreng, toss in a handful of bean sprouts or rings of spring onion, or both.
- Sprinkle with peanuts or coarsely chopped cashew nuts, with finely chopped fresh coriander or celery leaves, or, if you like it extra spicy, rings of chilli pepper.
- You can also serve it with prawn crackers. Or satay sauce. Or crispy fried onions. Or a simple cucumber salad. Or all of the above.

CLASSICS FOR ONE

Alone in the Kitchen with an Eggplant is a collection of essays compiled by Jenni Ferrari-Adler, in which twenty-six authors relate their experiences of eating alone. In one of the stories there's an older man living on his own who, when his daughter's friend invites him to join them for a meal, says, 'Oh, I couldn't. I've made lobster Newburg for dinner.'

Imagine: the man had gone to the market on his own, bought a lobster, cooked and dissected it, made stock from the shells and used this to make a sauce (along with butter, cream, sherry and eggs – lobster Newburg is an American adaptation of lobster Thermidor), folded the lobster meat into the sauce and spooned this heavenly mixture into a dish, ready to put in the oven that night. And not only had he done all of this with a great deal of pleasure, but he was also so looking forward to enjoying his classic tour de force that he turned down a dinner with his daughter for it. Of course, you might be tempted to say to someone like that, 'Come on, that lobster can wait until tomorrow – nothing beats having a meal with those you love.' But more than anything, I applaud this man. He has my respect! Now that's what I call taking good care of yourself.

Steak Béarnaise
with chips & salad

Preparation Time

30 minutes

For the chips

350 g floury potatoes, peeled

100 ml sunflower oil

For the Béarnaise sauce

1 small shallot, finely chopped

2 tbsp dry white wine

2 tbsp white wine vinegar

1 tbsp tarragon, finely chopped

80 g butter

1 egg yolk

lemon juice

1 tsp chervil, finely chopped

salt and freshly ground white
    pepper, to season

For the steak and salad

1 entrecôte of 150–175 g, at room
    temperature

½ tsp Dijon mustard

1 tsp red wine vinegar

1 tbsp olive oil

½ head butterhead lettuce or
    1 Little Gem, washed, dried,
    and torn into smaller pieces
    if necessary

coarse salt and freshly ground
    pepper, to season

Cut the potatoes into chips of around 1 x 1 cm thick. Rinse them under cold running water and pat them very dry in a clean tea towel. Heat the oil in a large frying pan over a high heat and add the chips in a single layer – they should sizzle when they hit the pan. Cover the pan, reduce the heat to medium and fry for 10 minutes, tossing them every now and then throughout the cooking time. Uncover, increase the heat to high and continue to cook until golden and crisp, tossing frequently, around another 10 minutes. Drain on kitchen paper and toss with some salt.

For the Béarnaise sauce, bring the shallot, wine, vinegar and half of the tarragon to the boil in a small saucepan over a high heat. Reduce the heat and simmer until there's about 1½ tablespoons of liquid left in the pan. Pour the liquid through a small strainer and set aside. Put the butter into the same saucepan and allow it to melt over a medium heat. Place a piece of kitchen paper in the strainer and carefully pour in the butter. You now have clarified butter.

Add the egg yolk and a small pinch of salt to the wine reduction in a small saucepan. Place the saucepan over a very low heat, with a heat diffuser under the pan; if you don't have a diffuser, suspend the saucepan over a larger pan of boiling water – but do not let it touch the boiling water. Gradually whisk in the clarified butter – first drop by drop and then increasing to a trickle – until you have a thick sauce. Taste and season with salt, freshly ground (white) pepper and lemon juice. To me, it should be nice and tart. Stir in the rest of the tarragon and the chervil to finish. Cover the sauce with a plate to keep it warm while you finish frying the chips, griddle the steak and toss the salad. This will also preheat your plate – yippee!

In the meantime, place a griddle pan over a high heat until it's red hot. Sprinkle the entrecôte with (coarse) salt and griddle on either side for 1–2 minutes for a rare steak. In a salad bowl, whisk together a dressing with the mustard, vinegar, olive oil and salt and pepper to taste. Add the lettuce and toss to coat.

Put the meat on the plate, add the chips, then take your plate, the bowl of salad and the pan with the sauce to the table (or wherever it is you plan to eat – in this case, bed might not be such a good idea …). The Béarnaise sauce is delicious not only with the meat, but also to dunk your chips in.

Sea bass in a salt crust

Although it might seem a bit extravagant to make this dish just for yourself, in fact it's ideal. This kind of one-person sea bass is much easier to pack in salt than a gigantic one meant to serve four. It's not that much work, and the result is phenomenal. The salt ensures that not even the tiniest molecule of flavour can escape. And what's more, you don't add a thing – this classic method allows the natural flavour of the fish to shine through. If you use white sea salt, you might have to dampen the salt a tiny bit first by wetting your hands and sprinkling it with a few drops of water. Grey sea salt is usually a little moister by nature and so sticks to the fish better.

Preparation Time

25 minutes

1 sea bass of around 400 g,
   cleaned, but with head and
   tail intact
1 kg coarse sea salt
2 sprigs each of thyme and
   rosemary (optional)
good-quality olive oil, for
   sprinkling

Preheat the oven to 200°C/180°C fan/400°F/Gas 6. Rinse the fish and pat it dry. Spread a thick layer of salt onto a baking sheet. Place the fish on top of the salt, and place the thyme and rosemary into the cavity of the fish and hermetically seal it with the rest of the salt – covering it completely so that only the tail sticks out. Bake in the oven for 20 minutes. Play it a little on the safe side – you can always put slightly underdone fish back in the oven, but you can't save overcooked fish.

Carefully break off the salt crust, then gently remove the skin from the fish and lift it out on to a board. Carefully remove the flesh to a plate and sprinkle with your very best olive oil.

Cheat's pizza Margherita

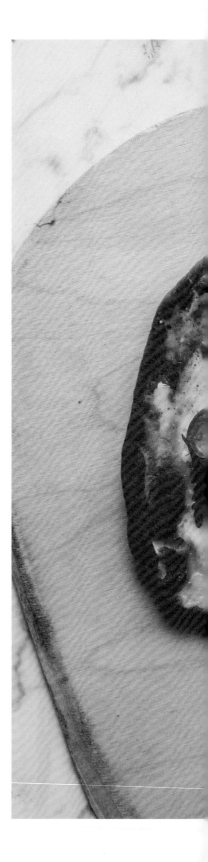

Preparation Time
15 minutes

200 g cherry tomatoes, cut in half
½ tsp red wine vinegar
olive oil
½ garlic clove, sliced paper-thin
a small pinch of chilli flakes

a few basil leaves
1 heat-and-serve naan
  or flatbread
1 small ball of (buffalo)
  mozzarella
a small handful of rocket leaves
salt and freshly ground pepper,
  to season

Preheat the oven to 200°C/180°C fan/400°F/Gas 6. Sprinkle
the cherry tomatoes with a pinch of salt and put them in
colander. Let them stand while the oven heats up, for around
10 minutes, then squeeze out as much liquid as you can.
Place them in a bowl, and mix in the vinegar, ½ tablespoon
of olive oil, the garlic, a small pinch of chilli flakes and a few
basil leaves.

Spread this mixture over the naan or flatbread. Tear the
mozzarella into pieces and put these on top of the tomatoes.
Bake for 7–10 minutes.

Toss the rocket with a splash of olive oil, some salt and lots
of freshly ground pepper. Take the pizza out of the oven and
sprinkle with the rocket to serve.

Solo chicken with rosemary & Roseval potatoes

Roast chicken. Go ahead, indulge yourself. Why deny yourself this kind of pleasure just because there's no one to share it with? If you buy a poussin, there's absolutely no need to deprive yourself – they're exactly the right size and weight for one person, which makes them the ideal solo bird. You can use thyme instead of rosemary, if you like.

Preparation Time

50 minutes

300 g Roseval potatoes, scrubbed
leaves from 1 sprig of rosemary
30 g butter, at room temperature
1 poussin, at room temperature
½ lemon, cut in half
olive oil, for drizzling
salt, to season

Preheat the oven to 180°C/160°C fan/350°F/Gas 4. Add the potatoes to a medium saucepan of salted water, bring to the boil and parboil for 5 minutes. Drain, let them sit for a bit to allow the steam to evaporate, then cut into large chunks.

Finely chop half of the rosemary leaves and mash these into the butter together with a pinch of salt. Put a bit of this rosemary butter into the bird's abdominal cavity. Add a piece of lemon. Rub the rest of the butter over the outside of the bird. Place the poussin in a baking dish and arrange the chunks of potato around it. Sprinkle the potatoes with the rest of the rosemary and some salt, then drizzle over a little olive oil. Tuck the other half of the lemon in among the potatoes. Bake for 35–45 minutes, until the chicken and potatoes are cooked through and golden brown.

Cassoulet

As a child, I thought tinned baked beans in tomato sauce were the ultimate treat. But a person's taste evolves over the years, and I now find the ready-made stuff far too sweet. Although I still regularly use beans from a tin – they're incredibly convenient – I now make my own, more grown-up version of baked beans: a kind of cassoulet, topped with bacon and crunchy breadcrumbs.

Preparation Time

15 minutes

olive oil, for frying

50 g smoked bacon, diced or cut
   into strips

1 large carrot, diced

1 celery stalk, diced

1 garlic clove, crushed

a pinch of chilli flakes

a pinch of dried thyme

½ glass of red wine (optional)

2 tomatoes, chopped

1 small tin (200–250 g) of haricot
   beans, drained and rinsed

½ tsp Dijon mustard

1 slice stale bread, whizzed
   into crumbs

salt and freshly ground pepper,
   to season

Heat a small splash of olive oil in a large frying pan and gently fry the bacon until crisp. Add the carrot and celery, and fry gently for another 5 minutes. Add the garlic, chilli flakes and thyme, and fry for another minute. Now pour in the red wine, if you're using it, and let it bubble for a bit. Add in the chopped tomatoes and let it all cook until it's a little bit sauce like. Add a small splash of water if necessary.

Finally, add the beans, the mustard and some salt and freshly ground pepper to taste, and heat for another few minutes while stirring.

Meanwhile, fry the breadcrumbs in a small frying pan in the a splash of olive oil over a medium–high heat until crisp and add a small pinch of salt. Put the beans in a bowl or deep plate, sprinkle with the breadcrumbs, and your cassoulet is ready.

10-minute pho

This is a one-person version of the renowned Vietnamese beef soup, which can be made in a flash. Gobble up the noodles using chopsticks as you hold the bowl next to your mouth and take the occasional sip of soup. Slurp as loudly as you like, because no one will hear you anyway. Just for fun, try doing this without slurping and see how much difference this makes. Eating is a multisensory feast, and (just like sex) noodle soup really does taste better when you make some noise.

Preparation Time

10 minutes

50 g rice vermicelli

a few drops of sesame oil

1 spring onion, sliced into matchsticks

1 tbsp coriander leaves, finely chopped

2 mint leaves, finely chopped (optional)

light soy sauce

350 ml beef stock (from a stock cube)

½ red chilli pepper, sliced

1 star anise

100 g lean beef mince

4–5 shiitake or button mushrooms, sliced

freshly ground pepper, to season

Put the rice vermicelli in a bowl, cover with boiling water and let it stand for 3 minutes. Turn into a colander, rinse the noodles with cold water and mix in a few drops of sesame oil. Put the noodles back in the bowl and add the spring onion and green herbs, 1 tablespoon of soy sauce and some freshly ground black pepper.

Meanwhile, bring the stock to the boil along with the chilli pepper and star anise. Knead 1 teaspoon of soy sauce into the mince and crumble this mixture into the pan with the stock. Then add the mushrooms. Turn the heat to low and let it simmer for 3 minutes. Pour the stock into the noodle bowl along with the meat and mushrooms. Add more soy sauce to taste, if you like. And don't forget to slurp.

Caesar salad with crispy pancetta & avocado

The secret of a good Caesar salad is, of course, the dressing. For this you boil an egg for 1 minute and then make a kind of mayonnaise with it along with crushed garlic, anchovies and Worcestershire sauce. If you happen to have some leftover chicken you can use that instead of the pancetta. Or use them both. It's your Caesar salad – you're chef and guest rolled into one.

Preparation Time

15 minutes

For the dressing

1 egg

½ garlic clove, crushed

2 anchovy fillets (from a tin or jar, drained)

½–1 tsp Dijon mustard

juice of ½ lemon

Worcestershire sauce, to taste

3–4 tbsp olive oil, plus extra for frying

For the salad

3 slices of pancetta

1 slice of (sourdough) bread, crust removed, then cubed

2 Little Gems, leaves separated

a small piece of Parmesan cheese

1 small ripe avocado, peeled and sliced

coarse salt and freshly ground pepper, to season

Bring some water to the boil in a saucepan and add the egg. Boil the egg for 1 minute and rinse immediately under cold running water to cool. Put the garlic and anchovies into a mortar along with a few grains of coarse salt and grind them smooth. Break in the egg, and stir in the mustard, a bit of lemon juice, Worcestershire sauce and some salt and freshly ground pepper to taste. Gradually whisk in 3–4 tablespoons of olive oil, as if you were making mayonnaise. Taste to see whether you need more salt, freshly ground pepper, lemon or Worcestershire sauce.

Heat the extra olive oil in a frying pan and slowly fry the pancetta until crisp over a medium–low heat. Drain on kitchen paper. Fry the bread cubes or croutons in the frying fat over a high heat until crisp, then drain on kitchen paper.

Place the lettuce leaves in a bowl or on a large plate, pour on two-thirds of the dressing and grate over a generous amount of Parmesan cheese. Toss with utensils or just use your hands, so that all of the leaves are lightly coated with dressing. Taste to see whether you want more dressing and add more, if necessary. Arrange the avocado, crispy pancetta and a scattering of croutons on top of the lettuce, and grind over a little more pepper.

Lamb chops with red wine & thyme sauce & green beans

In a French bistro, this would be served with fried potatoes, but fresh crusty (French) bread wouldn't go amiss here either. That takes zero effort, and it's wonderful for mopping up the buttery sauce.

Preparation Time

15 minutes

200 g green beans

2–3 lamb chops

olive oil, for frying

1 garlic clove, sliced paper thin

leaves from 2 sprigs of thyme

½ glass of red wine

75 ml lamb or chicken stock
  (from a cube or a jar)

35 g butter

salt and freshly ground pepper,
  to season

Cook the beans in a medium saucepan of salted boiling water for 3–4 minutes until just tender. Rinse them immediately under cold running water to cool.

Sprinkle the chops with salt and pepper on both sides. Heat the oil in a large frying pan over a high heat and fry for 2–2 ½ minutes on each side. Take the lamb chops out of the pan, put them on a plate and cover with tin foil to keep them warm. Put the pan back over the heat, and fry the garlic and thyme in the fat in which you fried the meat for 30 seconds. Pour in the wine and let it bubble for 1 minute. Add the stock and boil until it's slightly reduced, a further 2 minutes, then stir in the butter and add the cooked green beans. Heat the beans in the sauce, shaking the pan, for another 30 seconds, then spoon them on to the plate alongside the meat. Spoon the sauce over the lamb chops.

Steak tartare

Preparation Time

10 minutes

150 g fillet steak

½ shallot, finely chopped

1–2 tsp capers

2–3 small, sour, crunchy
   gherkins, finely chopped

3 sprigs of flat-leaf parsley, stems
   removed and finely chopped

1 egg yolk

½–1 tsp Dijon mustard

1 tbsp olive oil

Worcestershire sauce, to taste

Tabasco sauce, to taste

1 anchovy fillet (optional)

salt and freshly ground pepper,
   to season

Cut the meat into tiny cubes and stir in the shallot, capers, gherkins and parsley.

Put the egg yolk in a bowl and stir in the mustard. Whisk in the olive oil and season the dressing further with Worcestershire sauce, Tabasco sauce, salt and freshly ground pepper.

Mix the dressing into the meat, arrange the tartare in a nice little mound in the middle of your plate, and grind on a bit more pepper. You can top with an anchovy, if you like.

'PEOPLE WHO COOK JUST FOR THEMSELVES, THOSE ARE THE SMARTEST PEOPLE' **My butcher**

Risotto ai funghi

For mushroom risotto I like to use both dried and fresh mushrooms. Dried porcini mushrooms give the rice a deep savoury flavour you could never achieve with just fresh ones.

Preparation Time
40 minutes

5 g dried porcini mushrooms
  (funghi porcini)
olive oil, for frying
125 g chanterelles (or other
  mushrooms), large ones cut
  in half
1 celery stalk, sliced crossways
  into little arches
90 g risotto rice
a splash of dry red or white wine
  (optional)
300–400 ml hot vegetable or
  mushroom stock (from a cube
  or jar)
a small knob of butter
a small handful of grated
  Parmesan cheese
a small handful of flat-leaf
  parsley leaves, finely chopped
salt and freshly ground pepper,
  to season

Soak the dried mushrooms for 15 minutes in 100 ml lukewarm water. Heat 1 tablespoon of olive oil over a medium–high heat in a medium saucepan and cook the chanterelles until done. Season to taste with salt and pepper, remove from the pan and set aside. Squeeze the liquid from the soaked mushrooms and chop them until fairly fine. Strain the soaking liquid by pouring it through a strainer lined with a piece of kitchen paper.

Heat another splash of olive oil in the same pan and sauté the celery and the dried soaked porcini for 3 minutes. Add the rice to the pan and cook for another minute, stirring. Add the strained mushroom soaking liquid and stir occasionally as the liquid evaporates. If you're using it, add the wine to the pan now and allow everything to bubble until the liquid evaporates.

Then start adding the stock, one generous splash at a time. Before adding more stock, wait until the liquid is almost entirely absorbed. Continue to stir frequently. After about 16 minutes the rice should be nearly done, and the risotto should be fluid enough so that it ripples through the pan when you stir. Stir in the chanterelles, butter, Parmesan and parsley. Cover the pan and let the risotto rest for 2 minutes before digging in.

Too-good-to-share cheese fondue

Who says that cheese fondue is only for lovebirds? Believe me, it's also just fine on your own. And it doesn't always have to be the classic version made with Gruyère and Emmental. If you take a Camembert (the kind that comes in a little wooden box) and let it melt in the oven, you've got a ready-made cheese fondue in 20 minutes. Pour yourself a glass of chilled white wine and enjoy your own company. Oh, and you don't need a pricey raw-milk Camembert for this recipe, it works extremely well with a simple supermarket cheese.

Preparation Time

30 minutes

1 small Camembert in a
   wooden box
olive oil, for drizzling
a sprig of thyme
French bread, hard rolls or other
   crusty bread
raw vegetables (celery, carrots,
   cauliflower florets, Belgian
   endive spears, radishes etc.)

Preheat the oven to 220°C/200°C fan/425°F/Gas 7. Take the cheese out of its box and remove the paper or plastic wrapper. Put the Camembert back in the box. Cut a cross into the top of the cheese, drizzle with some olive oil and push in the sprig of thyme. Wrap the cheese, box and all, in a double layer of tin foil. Put the package into the oven for 20–25 minutes until the cheese is melted.

Meanwhile, put the bread and raw vegetables on a large plate. Unwrap the foil, set the wooden box with the melted Camembert in the middle and dunk away.

BE SWEET TO YOURSELF

When I was still very much struggling with my new life on my own (read: on quite a few mornings I wanted nothing more than to stay in bed all day long so I could wallow in self-pity), a psychologist friend told me she teaches her clients to think in terms of red and blue. Red stands for negative factors in your life; blue for positive. You often don't have much control over the red experiences, at least not as much as you'd like, but the blue experiences you can create yourself. By doing as many enjoyable things as you can, by creating small moments of happiness, you bring the red and blue into balance. I just thought I'd pass this idea along, because it helped me a lot.

Damn – if everything seems to be going wrong, I can still go out and do something nice. I can still make myself something good to eat. In other words, be sweet to yourself. Even on those days when everything else sucks, you can still have a little fun.

Blackberry mess

Preparation Time

5 minutes

a punnet of blackberries
1 large meringue or a few
   smaller ones
200 ml full-fat yoghurt
runny honey, to taste

In a bowl, crush the blackberries lightly with a fork – you don't need to mash them to a pulp, but they should bleed a little. Crumble in the meringue. Add the yoghurt to the bowl and drizzle over the honey. Fold the meringue crumbs and blackberries through the yoghurt. Tuck in before the meringues have a chance to get soft.

Instant mango–coconut ice cream

Hungry for ice cream but too lazy to go out and buy it? You can make some yourself in no time with a packet of frozen fruit. Of course, you can also use fruit other than mango, such as raspberries, blackberries or blueberries.

Preparation Time

5 minutes

150 g frozen mango chunks
1 small tin (170 ml) of coconut
  milk
a few fresh mint leaves
1 tbsp icing sugar
squeeze of lime juice

Put the frozen mango into the bowl of the food processor along with the coconut milk, mint leaves, icing sugar and a squeeze of lime juice. Process until the mixture is smooth and creamy. Taste, and add a little more sugar and/or lime juice, if desired. Put the ice cream into a bowl and dig in while it's cold.

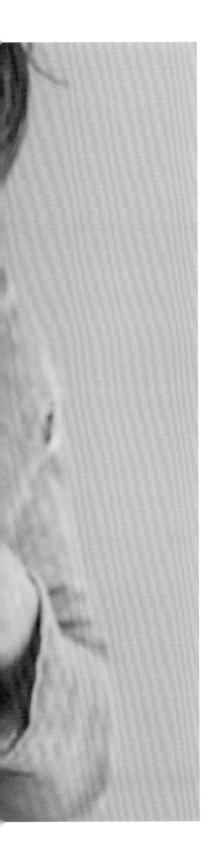

Lemon mug cake

Preparation Time

10 minutes

6 level tbsp plain flour

½ tsp baking powder

a small pinch of salt

1 egg

zest of ¼ lemon

2 tbsp white sugar

2 tbsp sunflower oil

6 tbsp milk

½ tbsp lemon curd

Chuck a few ingredients into a mug, mix and put it in the microwave. Mug cakes were invented for solo chefs with a sweet tooth. There's one thing you should know: eat your cake warm, because once it cools it will have lost all its charm.

Put the flour, baking powder, a small pinch of salt, egg, the lemon zest, sugar, oil and milk in a large microwave-proof mug, and stir until smooth. Bake the cake in the microwave on high for 2 minutes. Let it cool for a few minutes, top with a dollop of lemon curd and eat the warm cake out of the mug with a small spoon.

Warm apple tartlet with vanilla ice cream

An apple tart for one is a breeze when you use ready-made puff pastry. This is also wonderful with a spoonful of tart crème fraîche instead of the ice cream.

Preparation Time

25 minutes

a 12 x 12cm square of ready
   rolled puff pastry (freeze
   the remaining pastry for
   another day)
1 tbsp light brown sugar
1 tart apple, cored and
   thinly sliced
a small pinch of ground
   cinnamon
a few tiny flakes of butter
vanilla ice cream, to serve

Preheat the oven to 220°C/200°C fan/425°F/Gas 7. Place a piece of baking parchment on a baking sheet (this saves on clean-up) and add the puff-pastry square. Sprinkle with half of the sugar. Arrange the apple slices on top, either fanning them out or overlapping them in a line, like roof tiles. Sprinkle with the rest of the sugar and a small pinch of cinnamon. Top with the butter flakes and bake for 15–20 minutes until golden.

Eat the tartlet while still warm along with a generous scoop of vanilla ice cream.

Coffee–ricotta parfait

Preparation Time

5 minutes (+ at least 2 hours in
the freezer)

1 tsp instant coffee
1 tbsp caster sugar
125 g ricotta

Thoroughly combine the instant coffee, sugar and ricotta, taste and add more sugar, if you'd like. Line a small shallow dish with cling film. Spoon in the coffee–ricotta mixture and cover with more cling film. Freeze for at least 2 hours. Turn the coffee–ricotta parfait out on to a plate and dig in with a little spoon.

EVEN ON
THOSE
DAYS WHEN
EVERYTHING
ELSE SUCKS,
YOU CAN
STILL HAVE A
LITTLE FUN

La mousse au chocolat pour toi

Melt some chocolate, whip some cream and mix: making chocolate mousse can be that simple. If you like, you can flavour it with a tiny pinch of cinnamon or nutmeg, a little bit of finely grated orange zest or a tablespoon of your favourite liqueur.

Preparation Time

5 minutes

50 g dark (70% cocoa solids) chocolate, chopped

100 ml whipping cream

icing sugar, to taste (optional)

Place the chocolate in a microwave-proof bowl and heat in the microwave on high for 40–60 seconds to melt. If you don't have a microwave, you can also melt the chocolate by placing the bowl over a pan of simmering water (a bain-marie), making sure the base of the bowl is not touching the water. Whisk the cream until the peaks are almost stiff and fold in the melted chocolate. Sift in some icing sugar, if you like.

You can eat this at once, or let the mousse set in the fridge for an hour.

Rosemary–honey figs with Gorgonzola

Preparation Time
15 minutes

2–3 well-ripened figs
1 sprig of rosemary

olive oil, for greasing
runny honey, to drizzle
30 g Gorgonzola

Preheat the oven to 200°C/180°C fan/400°F/Gas 6. Slice the figs crossways down through the stem almost all the way to the bottom, then carefully push them open. Cut the sprig of rosemary into two or three pieces and tuck a piece into each fig. Put the figs in a shallow oiled baking dish. Drizzle each fig with a little honey and put them in the oven for 10–15 minutes until they're soft but still retain their shape. Eat the figs warm, with the Gorgonzola alongside.

A fantastic raspberry dessert

Preparation Time

10 minutes

½ tbsp flaked almonds

3 cantuccini

1 tbsp grappa (or any other kind of spirit/liqueur you enjoy)

a punnet of raspberries

60 ml whipping cream

runny honey, to taste

Toast the flaked almonds over a medium–high heat in a small dry frying pan until they start to brown, around 1–2 minutes. Break the cantuccini into pieces and put them in a wide glass. Sprinkle them with the grappa, then arrange half of the raspberries on top. Put the rest of the raspberries on a deep plate and mash well with a fork. Whip the cream until soft peaks form. Stir in the raspberry purée and sweeten with a little honey. Spoon into the glass and sprinkle with the toasted almonds.

Pear–yoghurt swirl

Preparation Time

5 minutes (+ 1 hour in the fridge)

1 small ripe eating pear

a few drops of lime juice

200 ml full-fat yoghurt

1 tbsp soft dark brown sugar

Peel and core the pear and dice the fruit. Toss with a little lime juice. Put the cubes of pear in a wide glass. Pour in the yoghurt and sprinkle on the brown sugar in an even layer. Put the glass in the fridge for an hour (longer is fine, too). Using a long-handled spoon, swirl the layer of melted sugar attractively through the yoghurt.

Tiramisu for one, please!

Preparation Time
10 minutes

25 g dark chocolate (a minimum
  of 70% cocoa solids)
75 g mascarpone

2 tbsp Marsala (or amaretto)
icing sugar, to taste
around 5 Lady fingers
  or sponge biscuits
a piping hot cup of espresso

**You'd have to be a real die-hard solo chef to make
yourself tiramisu. Whisking the eggs over a bain-marie,
building up the layers, chilling for hours – no, that
would be insane. But there are times when you suddenly
crave the kind of satisfying full-fat, alcohol-drenched
gratification that tiramisu has to offer. And so – ta-da! –
I present to you here this deconstructed version. It
contains all of the elements of tiramisu, and you can
make it in 10 minutes flat.**

Chop the chocolate, but not too fine – it's nice if it's still got
some bite. Put the mascarpone, 1 tablespoon of Marsala or
amaretto and the icing sugar to taste in a small bowl, and whip
with a small hand whisk until it's as light as possible. Fold in
the chopped chocolate. Spoon the mascarpone mixture on to
a small plate and place a few Lady fingers alongside. Make
yourself a strong cup of espresso and pour in the rest of the
Marsala or amaretto.

Sip your hot espresso as you nibble on Lady fingers dipped
in chocolate mascarpone.

SOLO
TREATS

One of the greatest advantages of cooking for yourself is that you can completely ditch 'the rules'. I mean, would you ever invite someone over for a meal and serve a potato gratin? Just a potato gratin and nothing else? You'd probably feel obliged to serve a piece of meat with it, or at least a salad. Would you dare to present your guests with a bowl of oatmeal and call it dinner? I know I wouldn't, even though I find that oatmeal sometimes really hits the spot. It might even be the ultimate comfort food.

As a solo chef, you truly don't need to take anyone else into account. You can completely and unashamedly surrender to your deepest desires, and be as eccentric or decadent as you like. There's no one around to comment. This chapter is an invitation to just go ahead and do your own thing.

Scrambled eggs and smoked salmon on toast make a fine dinner. A platter of oysters and a bottle of champagne in bed? Enjoy!

Oatmeal congee

Congee is the name for a Chinese dish consisting of rice porridge with savoury flavourings like soy sauce, ginger, spring onion and fermented vegetables or tofu. Although I love congee made with rice, I sometimes make a much quicker version using oatmeal. You might have to get used to the idea if you've always associated oatmeal with sweetness and breakfast, but believe me, that will all change once you've had your first bite.

Preparation Time

15 minutes

50 g porridge oats
a pinch of salt
1 spring onion, shredded
a piece of root ginger, finely
  chopped
a piece of red chilli pepper,
  finely sliced
a small handful of coriander
  leaves
toasted sesame oil, to season
Thai fish sauce and/or light
  soy sauce

Bring 350 ml water to the boil. Add the oats and a small pinch of salt. Turn down the heat to low and let it simmer for 10 minutes (or for the length of time given in the packet instructions), stirring occasionally with a spatula. Add a small splash of water if necessary, until the porridge has the desired consistency. Pour the oatmeal porridge into a bowl and sprinkle with the spring onion, ginger, chilli and coriander. Season further with a few drops of sesame oil and a small splash of fish or soy sauce (or, like I usually do, with both).

Parma ham–Taleggio toastie de luxe

Preparation Time
10 minutes

1 generous tbsp grated
 Parmesan cheese
1 tbsp mayonnaise
1 tsp Dijon mustard
2 large slices of bread
 (sourdough, if you like)

butter, for spreading
2 slices Parma ham
75 g Taleggio cheese, sliced
salt and freshly ground pepper,
 to season
1 tbsp olive oil, if using a
 frying pan

**Is a toastie dinner? Sure it is – but then it should
preferably be one that's especially delectable.
What makes this one so luscious is not only the Parma
ham and Taleggio but also the sauce made from
mayonnaise, mustard and Parmesan, with which you
spread the bread first. In addition to making a good
dinner, this toastie also makes a good anti-hangover
breakfast.**

Stir the Parmesan into the mayonnaise and add the mustard,
salt and freshly ground pepper to taste. Spread one side of the
slices of bread with butter and the other side with the mayo
mixture. Top one of the bread slices, mayo-side up, with the
Parma ham and Taleggio, then cover this with the other slice
of bread, mayo-side down. Cook the toastie in a toastie maker
(or in a frying pan in the olive oil, over a medium–high heat,
for 3–5 minutes on each side, until golden and crisp on the
outside and oozing in the middle. Place something heavy such
as a griddle plan on top of the toastie so that it gets pressed
down a bit).

'IT IS THE PRIVILEGE OF LONELINESS; IN PRIVACY ONE MAY DO AS ONE CHOOSES'

Mrs Dalloway, **Virginia Woolf**

Scrambled eggs, griddled asparagus & salmon on toast

In the United States they call this 'brinner', or breakfast for dinner. There, it's all the rage to eat something you'd usually have for breakfast as your evening meal. Funny, because that means this classic dish of scrambled eggs with asparagus, toast and salmon is suddenly ultra-hip.

Preparation Time

10 minutes

150 g green asparagus tips

olive oil

2–3 slices of bread

2 eggs

25 g butter

75 g smoked salmon

½ box of garden cress

salt and freshly ground pepper,
 to season

Place a griddle pan over a high heat until it's hot as blazes. Toss the asparagus tips with some olive oil and griddle for 5–7 minutes until char marks have formed. Sprinkle with a small pinch of salt. Toast the bread. Whisk the eggs gently in a bowl with a little salt and freshly ground pepper.

Melt two-thirds of the butter in a small heavy-based frying pan over a low heat. Pour in the eggs and allow them to set gradually while you stir constantly but gently with a spatula. Remove the pan from the heat as soon as the eggs start to hold their shape. Stir in the rest of the butter. Spoon the scrambled eggs on to a plate, add the griddled asparagus and salmon alongside and snip the cress over the eggs. Eat with the toast.

Stir-fried prawns with harissa mayo

Because you should never underestimate the pleasure of eating with your hands and then licking your fingers clean: prawns with mayo.

Preparation Time

10 minutes

3 tbsp mayonnaise

1–2 tsp harissa paste

rice or peanut oil, for frying

300 g large raw prawns,
  unpeeled

a pinch of coarse sea salt

Put the mayonnaise into a bowl and stir in as much harissa as tastes good to you.

Heat a wok over a high heat until it starts to smoke. Add a small splash of oil. Add the prawns and a pinch of coarse salt to the wok. Stir-fry for 3 minutes until they're just done and have turned nice and pink and are slightly charred. Peel the prawns and dunk them in the harissa mayo.

Potato gratin with a whole load of cheese

Parboil the potatoes, put them into a baking dish, add lots of cream and lots of cheese, and bake for half an hour. This potato gratin is rich but irresistible. You can make a green salad to go along with it, if you like, but you don't have to. (Just so you know …)

Preparation Time

45 minutes

400 g waxy potatoes, peeled
    and thinly sliced
butter, for greasing
125 ml crème fraîche
1 garlic clove, crushed
125 g grated Gruyère cheese
salt and freshly ground pepper,
    to season

Preheat the oven to 180°C/160°C fan/350°F/Gas 4. Bring a medium saucepan with plenty of salted water to the boil and parboil the potato slices for 8 minutes. Butter a small baking dish. Drain the potatoes and tip them into the baking dish. Mix the crème fraîche with the garlic, half of the cheese, a pinch of salt and lots of freshly ground pepper, and pour over the potatoes. Sprinkle with the rest of the cheese and bake for 25–30 minutes until bubbling and slightly browned. Let the gratin rest for 5 minutes or so before you attack.

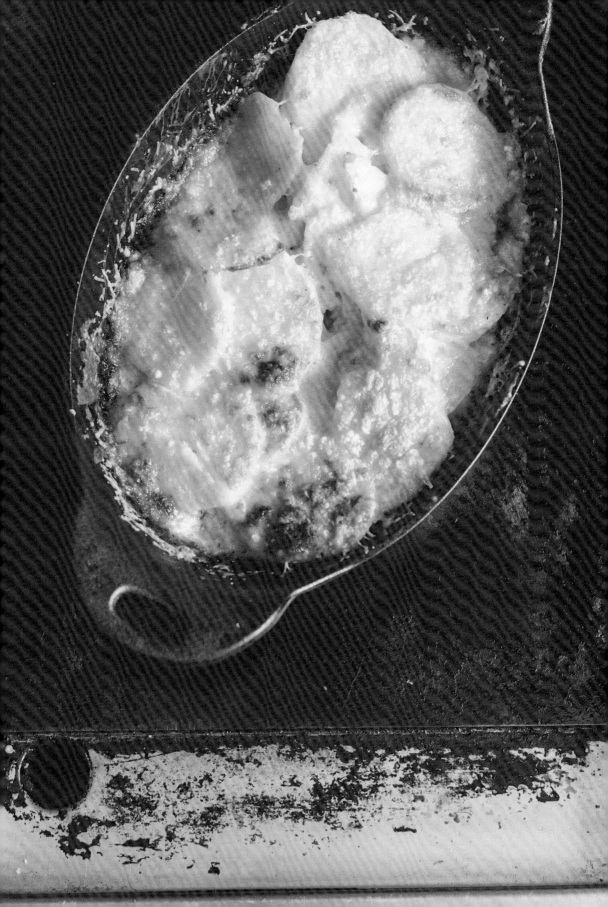

Calf's liver sans etiquette

Fried calf's liver, yum. My children don't like it, which is exactly why I love making it when it's just me. Add some bread, and that's it. (After all, onion is also a vegetable …) Oh, and because no one's watching anyway, I actually think this tastes best if you eat it straight from the pan, dragging your bread through the jus to get the very last drop. We'll bow to the rules of etiquette some other time.

Preparation Time

20 minutes

olive oil, for frying

40 g butter

1 large onion, sliced into rings

150 g calf's liver, sliced on the
  diagonal into 5 mm strips

a splash of dry Marsala
  (or sherry)

a small handful of flat-leaf
  parsley leaves, finely chopped
  (optional)

a wedge of lemon

salt and freshly ground pepper,
  to season

bread, to serve

Heat the olive oil and a bit (10 g) of the butter in a frying pan over a high heat. Add the onion and fry for 3 minutes while stirring. Sprinkle with a little salt, turn down the heat to medium–low, cover the pan and allow the onion to fry gently for 10–15 minutes, until it starts to caramelise. Remove the lid, turn the heat back up to high and fry the onion rings for 2 more minutes until they're nice and brown. Remove from the pan and set aside.

Add the rest of the butter to the pan and fry the liver slices over a high heat, turning regularly, until they're brown on both sides. This has to happen very fast, in around 1 ½ minutes, or the meat will be dry and the thrill will be gone. After 1 minute, return the onion to the pan, sprinkle everything with salt and freshly ground pepper, and deglaze with Marsala (or sherry). Let it bubble for another 15 seconds, then sprinkle with parsley, if using, and a squeeze of lemon juice.

Party for one

There's this saying in Dutch: 'Life is a party, but you have to hang up the bunting yourself.' So very true, dear solo chef. Now go ahead and open that good bottle of wine, put on your favourite tunes and dance around the room. Then nestle down on the sofa with a plate full of finger food. You don't need to spend much time in the kitchen at all. If you shop strategically, you'll be all set to go to your party for one.

Some suggestions

Preparation Time

15 minutes each

Solo mezze

Flatbread with olive oil and
  dukkah for dipping
hummus with crudités for
  dipping
tabbouleh
a piece of creamy feta
a small handful of olives
cooked beets (chopped) with a
  dressing of balsamic vinegar,
  lemon juice, olive oil, salt,
  pepper and thyme, topped with
  a spoonful of cottage cheese
griddled aubergine slices with
  a dressing of lemon, olive oil,
  salt and pepper sprinkled with
  pomegranate seeds, walnuts
  and fresh mint

Solo tapas

pan con tomate: toasted bread
  spread with half a tomato and
  sprinkled with olive oil
Spanish sliced meats (for
  example, Serrano ham
  and chorizo)
a small handful of olives
smoked almonds
marinated anchovies
slices of Manchego and
  quince jelly
griddled Belgian endive (cut
  into quarters and griddle in a
  griddle pan) with a dressing
  of orange juice, olive oil, salt,
  pepper and thyme, sprinkled
  with crumbled blue cheese
button mushrooms sautéed with
  garlic, deglazed with sherry,
  then sprinkled with salt, pepper
  and parsley

Solo Nordic nibbles

toasted bread or rye bread,
  or crackers
gravadlax (marinated salmon)
  with a spoonful of crème fraîche
prawns with a squeeze of lemon
  and some finely chopped dill
herring with raw onion
sliced cooked ham and/or liver
  pâté with sour gherkins and/
  or a spoonful of chutney (or, if
  you like it sweet, a spoonful of
  berry jam)
Swedish meatballs (from IKEA,
  also available in supermarkets)
thin slices or small cubes of
  cucumber in a dressing of
  white wine vinegar, salt, a
  small pinch of sugar and finely
  chopped dill
diced cooked beetroot, tossed
  in mayonnaise, crème fraîche,
  lemon juice, salt and pepper

Oysters, Champagne & a good book

Enough already. No more phone calls, WhatsApps, Facebook updates, Instagram pics or any other form of oh-so-warm-and-sociable-but-at-times-incredibly-irritating forms of distraction. Cool white sheets, cold champagne, oysters and a good book. This is me time.

Preparation Time

15 minutes

1 small shallot
3 tbsp red wine vinegar
1 lime
at least a dozen oysters
slices of white bread
Tabasco sauce
butter, for spreading
a bottle of chilled Champagne

Peel the shallot and cut it into the thinnest-possible slices. Put into a small bowl with the vinegar and grate a tiny bit of lime zest over the mixture. Let it stand for at least 10 minutes.

Meanwhile, cut open the oysters. Slice the creatures loose and remove any grit. Place the oysters on a large platter and put this on a tray. Toast the bread. Cut the lime into wedges. Place the bowl with the shallots in vinegar next to the oysters, along with a bottle of Tabasco, the toast, butter, a pepper mill and the lime wedges. And, of course, the bottle of Champagne and a Champagne flute. Take everything to bed with you, along with a good book, and enjoy your freedom. Solo is the new togetherness.

A WORD OF THANKS

I can do a great many things on my own, but a book? That takes a team. And what a team it was.

First of all, I would like to thank my publisher, Joost Nijsen. Years ago, Joost approached me to ask whether I wanted to write a cookbook for singles. I thought it was an excellent idea straight away. But, alas, no time. And, to be honest, in the midst of my busy family life, I also didn't have quite enough experience of the subject matter. Life, however, can take unexpected turns, and so, Joost, here you have it: *Solo Food*. Our first project together. I'm already looking forward to the next one.

I discovered that only nice people work at Joost's publishing company. Although Podium might be located in the middle of nowhere – in any case, it's a helluva long cycle ride from town – once you step inside, it's like sinking down into a warm bath. Thank you, Willemijn Lindhout, Trisha de Lang and Susanne ter Smitten, for your enthusiasm, encouragement and boundless dedication. And for the ice creams during our sweltering brainstorming sessions.

Working with Monique Mulder, Paul van Ravestein and Erick de Jong from Mattmo design agency was just as pleasurable. Without the efforts of these creative spirits, this book would most certainly not have looked as wonderful as it does. Thank you, Monique, Paul and Erick. And I would certainly also like to thank photographer

Floortje van Essen-Ingen Housz and stylist Caroline Lamet. What a good time we had during the photo shoots, girls, and what wonderful images they produced.

Photographer Sean Fitzpatrick shot not only the portrait of me on the Dutch cover, he also made a lovely little video about *Solo Food*. Thx, Sean. Jonah Freud thought along with me how to structure the book. Thank you, dear Jonah. I'm very grateful to DOK cookware in The Hague for letting me use lots of their tableware.

So many people, and all of them essential to bringing this book into being. Not only could I not have done this on my own but it would also have been a lot less inspiring and a lot less fun. And then there are all of those dear friends and family members who pulled me through the year of my divorce, who comforted me, helped me, encouraged me and who made me laugh through my tears. I am more grateful to these people than words can say.

Looking back, I can only conclude that, although I might be travelling through life solo, a person never has to go it alone. And how great is that?

Janneke Vreugdenhil

INDEX

A

All-round chicken soup 102–3
almonds
  A fantastic raspberry dessert
    160
  Pesto at your fingertips 115
  Quinotto with fennel, almonds
    and avocado 78
anchovies
  Caesar salad with crispy
    pancetta and avocado 136
  Orecchiette with Tenderstem
    broccoli, anchovies and
    fennel seed 90
  Polenta pizza with blistered
    cherry tomatoes and
    anchovies 57
  Steak tartare 139
apples
  Warm apple tartlet with
    vanilla ice cream 152
asparagus
  Scrambled eggs, griddled
    asparagus and salmon on
    toast 171
aubergines
  Quick aubergine and lamb
    curry with warm naan 82
  Ratatouille 116–17
avocados
  Caesar salad with crispy
    pancetta and avocado 136
  Griddled white tuna with
    cucumber, avocado and
    ginger salad 38
  Quinotto with fennel, almonds
    and avocado 78

B

bacon
  Basic nasi goreng 120–1
  Caesar salad with crispy
    pancetta and avocado 136
  Cassoulet 131
Basic nasi goreng 120–1
basil
  Cheat's pizza Margherita 128
  Pesto at your fingertips 115
  Polenta pizza with blistered
    cherry tomatoes and
    anchovies 57
  Ridiculously easy spaghetti
    caprese 34
  Spaghetti with cherry
    tomatoes, nutmeg and
    ricotta 88
beans
  Cassoulet 131
  Chilli con everything 100
  Salad of butter beans, tinned
    tuna and shaved fennel 44
Béarnaise sauce 124–5
beef
  Chilli con everything 100
  Chinese egg noodles with
    steak and oyster sauce 73
  Comforting little casseroles
    104–5
  Good old steak sandwich 47
  Steak Béarnaise with chips
    and salad 124–5
  Steak tartare 139
  10-minute pho 132

beer
  Comforting little casseroles
    104–5
Best-ever fried rice 71
biscuits
  A fantastic raspberry dessert
    160
black beans
  Chilli con everything 100
Blackberry mess 146
Bowl of rice with Chinesey
  vegetables 96
bread
  Caesar salad with crispy
    pancetta and avocado 136
  Cassoulet 131
  Cheat's pizza Margherita 128
  Good old steak sandwich 47
  Oysters, Champagne and a
    good book 181
  Parma ham-Taleggio toastie
    de luxe 169
  Quick aubergine and lamb
    curry with warm naan 82
  Scrambled eggs, griddled
    asparagus and salmon on
    toast 171
  Spicy lamb pittas with
    hummus and garlicky
    yoghurt 30
  Too-good-to-share cheese
    fondue 142
broad beans
  Gnocchi with broad beans,
    brown butter and crispy
    sage 81

broccoli
  Bowl of rice with Chinesey
    vegetables 96
  Orecchiette with Tenderstem
    broccoli, anchovies and
    fennel seed 90
brown butter
  Gnocchi with broad beans,
    brown butter and crispy
    sage 81
butter beans
  Salad of butter beans, tinned
    tuna and shaved fennel 44
butternut squash
  Roasted squash and carrot
    soup 106–7

C
cabbage
  Basic nasi goreng 120–1
Caesar salad with crispy
    pancetta and avocado 136
cakes
  Lemon mug cake 151
Calf's liver sans etiquette 176
Camembert cheese
  Too-good-to-share cheese
    fondue 142
cantuccini
  A fantastic raspberry dessert
    160
capers
  Salad of butter beans, tinned
    tuna and shaved fennel 44
  Steak tartare 139
  Warm salad of new potatoes
    and peppered mackerel 86
carrots
  Cassoulet 131
  Roasted squash and carrot
    soup 106–7
  Spicy lentil soup with yoghurt
    and rocket 66
cashew nuts
  Bowl of rice with Chinesey
    vegetables 96

casseroles
  Comforting little casseroles
    104–5
  Pork loin stewed with red
    wine and bay leaves 111
Cassoulet 131
celery
  Pasta sauce with fresh
    sausage and fennel seeds
    110
  Pork loin stewed with red
    wine and bay leaves 111
Champagne
  Oysters, Champagne and a
    good book 181
chanterelles
  Risotto ai funghi 141
Cheat's pizza Margherita 128
cheese
  Baked sweet potato with
    olives, feta and chilli 50
  Caesar salad with crispy
    pancetta and avocado 136
  Cheat's pizza Margherita 128
  Coffee-ricotta parfait 153
  Frittata with red onion, baby
    kale and goat's cheese 35
  Mashed potatoes 104–5
  Parma ham-Taleggio toastie
    de luxe 169
  Pesto at your fingertips 115
  Potato gratin with a whole
    load of cheese 174
  Ridiculously easy spaghetti
    caprese 34
  Risotto ai funghi 141
  Rosemary-honey figs with
    Gorgonzola 158
  Soft polenta with mushrooms
    and spinach 54
  Spaghetti with cherry
    tomatoes, nutmeg and
    ricotta 88
  Too-good-to-share cheese
    fondue 142
  Warm lentil salad with grilled
    goat's cheese 64

chicken
  All-round chicken soup 102–3
  Green curry with chicken
    and peas 85
  Marcella's sugo 112–13
  Solo chicken with rosemary
    and Roseval potatoes 130
  Surinamese masala chicken
    118
chilli peppers
  Baked sweet potato with
    olives, feta and chilli 50
  Basic nasi goreng 120–1
  Bowl of rice with Chinesey
    vegetables 96
  Cassoulet 131
  Cheat's pizza Margherita 128
  Chilli con everything 100
  Cod in ginger-tomato sauce
    with gremolata and rice 68
  Griddled white tuna with
    cucumber, avocado and
    ginger salad 38
  Oatmeal congee 166
  Pasta aglio olio my way 84
  Pasta sauce with fresh
    sausage and fennel seeds
    110
  Surinamese masala chicken
    118
  10-minute pho 132
Chinese egg noodles with
    steak and oyster sauce 73
Chips 124–5
chocolate
  Chilli con everything 100
  La mousse au chocolat pour
    toi 154
  Tiramisu for one 163
chorizo
  A kind of pisto Manchego 29
  Mash with baby kale and
    chorizo 60
coconut milk
  Green curry with chicken
    and peas 85
  Instant mango-coconut ice
    cream 148

Sweet potato soup with coconut and fresh coriander 53

Cod in ginger-tomato sauce with gremolata and rice 68

coffee
Coffee-ricotta parfait 153
Tiramisu for one 163

Cold noodle salad with cucumber and sashimi salmon 74

Comforting little casseroles 104–5

Congee, oatmeal 166

coriander
Green curry with chicken and peas 85
Oatmeal congee 166
Quick aubergine and lamb curry with warm naan 82
Quinotto with fennel, almonds and avocado 78
Sweet potato soup with coconut and fresh coriander 53
10-minute pho 132

courgettes
Courgette soup with tarragon 93
A kind of pisto Manchego 29
Ratatouille 116–17

couscous
Lemon couscous with salmon and cherry tomatoes 42

cream
A fantastic raspberry dessert 160
La mousse au chocolat pour toi 154

crème fraîche
Potato gratin with a whole load of cheese 174

cress
Scrambled eggs, griddled asparagus and salmon on toast 171
Warm salad of new potatoes and peppered mackerel 86

cucumber
Cold noodle salad with cucumber and sashimi salmon 74
Griddled white tuna with cucumber, avocado and ginger salad 38

curry
Basic nasi goreng 120–1
Green curry with chicken and peas 85
Quick aubergine and lamb curry with warm naan 82
Surinamese masala chicken 118
Sweet potato soup with coconut and fresh coriander 53

E

egg noodles
Chinese egg noodles with steak and oyster sauce 73

eggs
Frittata with red onion, baby kale and goat's cheese 35
A kind of pisto Manchego 29
Mashed potatoes 104–5
Patatas a lo pobre 63
Scrambled eggs, griddled asparagus and salmon on toast 171
Soft polenta with mushrooms and spinach 54
Steak tartare 139

F

A fantastic raspberry dessert 160

fennel
Quinotto with fennel, almonds and avocado 78
Salad of butter beans, tinned tuna and shaved fennel 44

fennel seeds
Orecchiette with Tenderstem broccoli, anchovies and fennel seed 90

Pasta sauce with fresh sausage and fennel seeds 110

feta cheese
Baked sweet potato with olives, feta and chilli 50

figs
Rosemary-honey figs with Gorgonzola 158

fish
Marcella's sugo 112–13
see also salmon, tuna etc

fondue
Too-good-to-share cheese fondue 142

freezers 99

Frittata with red onion, baby kale and goat's cheese 35

G

garden cress
Scrambled eggs, griddled asparagus and salmon on toast 171
Warm salad of new potatoes and peppered mackerel 86

garlic
Basic nasi goreng 120–1
Pasta aglio olio my way 84
Patatas a lo pobre 63
Pesto at your fingertips 115
Pork loin stewed with red wine and bay leaves 111
Ratatouille 116–17
Spicy lamb pittas with hummus and garlicky yoghurt 30
Surinamese masala chicken 118

gherkins
Steak tartare 139

ginger
All-round chicken soup 102–3
Basic nasi goreng 120–1
Best-ever fried rice 71
Bowl of rice with Chinesey vegetables 96

Cod in ginger-tomato sauce with gremolata and rice 68

Griddled white tuna with cucumber, avocado and ginger salad 38

Gnocchi with broad beans, brown butter and crispy sage 81

goat's cheese
  Frittata with red onion, baby kale and goat's cheese 35
  Warm lentil salad with grilled goat's cheese 64

Good old steak sandwich 47

Gorgonzola
  Rosemary-honey figs with Gorgonzola 158

grappa
  A fantastic raspberry dessert 160

gratins
  Potato gratin with a whole load of cheese 174

green beans
  Lamb chops with red wine and thyme sauce and green beans 138

Green curry with chicken and peas 85

gremolata
  Cod in ginger-tomato sauce with gremolata and rice 68

Gruyère cheese
  Potato gratin with a whole load of cheese 174

H

ham
  A kind of pisto Manchego 29
  Parma ham-Taleggio toastie de luxe 169

haricot beans
  Cassoulet 131
  Chilli con everything 100

harissa paste
  Spicy lamb pittas with hummus and garlicky yoghurt 30

Stir-fried prawns with harissa mayo 172

hazelnuts
  Pesto at your fingertips 115

honey
  Rosemary-honey figs with Gorgonzola 158

hummus
  Spicy lamb pittas with hummus and garlicky yoghurt 30

I

ice cream
  Coffee-ricotta parfait 153
  Instant mango-coconut ice cream 148
  Warm apple tartlet with vanilla ice cream 152

Indonesian fried rice 120–1

ingredients 23

Instant mango-coconut ice cream 148

K

kaffir lime leaves
  All-round chicken soup 102–3

kale
  Frittata with red onion, baby kale and goat's cheese 35
  Mash with baby kale and chorizo 60

kidney beans
  Chilli con everything 100

A kind of pisto Manchego 29

L

lamb
  Lamb chops with red wine and thyme sauce and green beans 138
  Marcella's sugo 112–13
  Quick aubergine and lamb curry with warm naan 82
  Spicy lamb pittas with hummus and garlicky yoghurt 30

leeks
  Basic nasi goreng 120–1

leftovers 49

lemon
  Lemon couscous with salmon and cherry tomatoes 42
  Lemon mug cake 151
  Solo chicken with rosemary and Roseval potatoes 130

lemongrass
  All-round chicken soup 102–3

lentils
  Spicy lentil soup with yoghurt and rocket 66
  Warm lentil salad with grilled goat's cheese 64

lettuce
  Caesar salad with crispy pancetta and avocado 136
  Good old steak sandwich 47
  Steak Béarnaise with chips and salad 124–5

lime
  Green curry with chicken and peas 85
  Oysters, Champagne and a good book 181
  Sweet potato soup with coconut and fresh coriander 53

liver
  Calf's liver sans etiquette 176

M

mackerel
  Warm salad of new potatoes and peppered mackerel 86

mangos
  Instant mango-coconut ice cream 148

Marcella's sugo 112–13

Marsala
  Calf's liver sans etiquette 176
  Tiramisu for one 163

mascarpone
  Tiramisu for one 163

Mash with baby kale and chorizo 60

Mashed potatoes 104–5
mayonnaise
　Good old steak sandwich 47
　Parma ham-Taleggio toastie
　　de luxe 169
　Stir-fried prawns with harissa
　　mayo 172
meringue
　Blackberry mess 146
mezze 178
Miso soup with noodles,
　shiitake mushrooms,
　spinach and an egg 32
La mousse au chocolat pour
　toi 154
mozzarella cheese
　Cheat's pizza Margherita 128
　Ridiculously easy spaghetti
　　caprese 34
mug cake, lemon 151
mushrooms
　Bowl of rice with Chinesey
　　vegetables 96
　Miso soup with noodles,
　　shiitake mushrooms,
　　spinach and an egg 32
　Risotto ai funghi 141
　Soft polenta with mushrooms
　　and spinach 54
　10-minute pho 132

N
naan bread
　Cheat's pizza Margherita 128
　Quick aubergine and lamb
　　curry with warm naan 82
Nasi goreng 120–1
noodles
　Chinese egg noodles with
　　steak and oyster sauce 73
　Cold noodle salad with
　　cucumber and sashimi
　　salmon 74
　Miso soup with noodles,
　　shiitake mushrooms,
　　spinach and an egg 32
　10-minute pho 132
Nordic nibbles 178

O
Oatmeal congee 166
olive oil
　Pesto at your fingertips 115
olives
　Baked sweet potato with
　　olives, feta and chilli 50
　Polenta pizza with blistered
　　cherry tomatoes and
　　anchovies 57
onions
　Basic nasi goreng 120–1
　Calf's liver sans etiquette 176
　Chilli con everything 100
　Comforting little casseroles
　　104–5
　Frittata with red onion, baby
　　kale and goat's cheese 35
　A kind of pisto Manchego 29
　Marcella's sugo 112–13
　Pasta sauce with fresh
　　sausage and fennel seeds
　　110
　Patatas a lo pobre 63
　Polenta pizza with blistered
　　cherry tomatoes and
　　anchovies 57
　Pork loin stewed with red
　　wine and bay leaves 111
　Ratatouille 116–17
　Roasted squash and carrot
　　soup 106–7
　Surinamese masala chicken
　　118
　see also shallots; spring
　　onions
Orecchiette with Tenderstem
　broccoli, anchovies and
　fennel seed 90
oyster mushrooms
　Bowl of rice with Chinesey
　　vegetables 96
oyster sauce
　Chinese egg noodles with
　　steak and oyster sauce 73
Oysters, Champagne and a
　good book 181

P
pancetta
　Caesar salad with crispy
　　pancetta and avocado 136
parfait, Coffee-ricotta 153
Parma ham-Taleggio toastie
　de luxe 169
Parmesan cheese
　Parma ham-Taleggio toastie
　　de luxe 169
　Pesto at your fingertips 115
　Risotto ai funghi 141
　Soft polenta with mushrooms
　　and spinach 54
parsley
　Calf's liver sans etiquette 176
　Cod in ginger-tomato sauce
　　with gremolata and rice 68
　Patatas a lo pobre 63
　Risotto ai funghi 141
　Steak tartare 139
Party for one 178
pasta
　Marcella's sugo 112–13
　Orecchiette with Tenderstem
　　broccoli, anchovies and
　　fennel seed 90
　Pasta aglio olio my way 84
　Pasta sauce with fresh
　　sausage and fennel seeds
　　110
　Ridiculously easy spaghetti
　　caprese 34
　Spaghetti with cherry
　　tomatoes, nutmeg and
　　ricotta 88
　Tagliatelle with prawns and
　　smoky whisky-tomato sauce
　　41
　Patatas a lo pobre 63
Pear-yoghurt swirl 160
peas
　Green curry with chicken
　　and peas 85
　Lemon couscous with salmon
　　and cherry tomatoes 42
peppers
　A kind of pisto Manchego 29

Ratatouille 116–17
see also chilli peppers
Pesto at your fingertips 115
Pho, 10-minute 132
Pisto Manchego 29
pitta breads
　Spicy lamb pittas with
　　hummus and garlicky
　　yoghurt 30
pizza
　Cheat's pizza Margherita 128
　Marcella's sugo 112–13
　Polenta pizza with blistered
　　cherry tomatoes and
　　anchovies 57
polenta
　Polenta pizza with blistered
　　cherry tomatoes and
　　anchovies 57
　Soft polenta with mushrooms
　　and spinach 54
porcini mushrooms
　Risotto ai funghi 141
pork
　Basic nasi goreng 120–1
　Pork loin stewed with red
　　wine and bay leaves 111
potatoes
　Courgette soup with tarragon
　　93
　Mash with baby kale and
　　chorizo 60
　Mashed potatoes 104–5
　Patatas a lo pobre 63
　Potato gratin with a whole
　　load of cheese 174
　Solo chicken with rosemary
　　and Roseval potatoes 130
　Steak Béarnaise with chips
　　and salad 124–5
　Warm salad of new potatoes
　　and peppered mackerel 86
poussin
　Solo chicken with rosemary
　　and Roseval potatoes 130
prawns
　Stir-fried prawns with harissa
　　mayo 172

Tagliatelle with prawns and
　smoky whisky-tomato sauce
　41

Q
Quick aubergine and lamb
　curry with warm naan 82
quinoa
　Quinotto with fennel, almonds
　　and avocado 78

R
ramen noodles
　Miso soup with noodles,
　　shiitake mushrooms,
　　spinach and an egg 32
raspberries
　A fantastic raspberry dessert
　　160
Ratatouille 116–17
rice
　Basic nasi goreng 120–1
　Best-ever fried rice 71
　Bowl of rice with Chinesey
　　vegetables 96
　Cod in ginger-tomato sauce
　　with gremolata and rice 68
　Green curry with chicken
　　and peas 85
　Risotto ai funghi 141
rice vermicelli
　10-minute pho 132
ricotta
　Coffee-ricotta parfait 153
　Spaghetti with cherry
　　tomatoes, nutmeg and
　　ricotta 88
Ridiculously easy spaghetti
　caprese 34
Risotto ai funghi 141
rocket
　Cheat's pizza Margherita 128
rosemary
　Pork loin stewed with red
　　wine and bay leaves 111
　Roasted squash and carrot
　　soup 106–7

Rosemary-honey figs with
　Gorgonzola 158
Solo chicken with rosemary
　and Roseval potatoes 130

S
sage
　Gnocchi with broad beans,
　　brown butter and crispy
　　sage 81
salads
　Caesar salad with crispy
　　pancetta and avocado 136
　Cucumber, avocado and
　　ginger salad 38
　Salad of butter beans, tinned
　　tuna and shaved fennel 44
　Steak Béarnaise with chips
　　and salad 124–5
　Warm lentil salad with grilled
　　goat's cheese 64
　Warm salad of new potatoes
　　and peppered mackerel 86
salmon
　Cold noodle salad with
　　cucumber and sashimi
　　salmon 74
　Lemon couscous with salmon
　　and cherry tomatoes 42
　see also smoked salmon
salt
　Sea bass in a salt crust 126
sandwiches
　Good old steak sandwich 47
　Parma ham-Taleggio toastie
　　de luxe 169
sauces
　Béarnaise sauce 124–5
　Marcella's sugo 112–13
　Pasta sauce with fresh
　　sausage and fennel seeds
　　110
　Pesto at your fingertips 115
　Red wine and thyme sauce
　　138

sausages
   Pasta sauce with fresh
      sausage and fennel seeds
      110
   see also chorizo
Scrambled eggs, griddled
      asparagus and salmon on
      toast 171
Sea bass in a salt crust 126
sesame seeds
   Cold noodle salad with
      cucumber and sashimi
      salmon 74
shallots
   Basic nasi goreng 120–1
shiitake mushrooms
   Miso soup with noodles,
      shiitake mushrooms,
      spinach and an egg 32
   10-minute pho 132
smoked mackerel
   Warm salad of new potatoes
      and peppered mackerel 86
smoked salmon
   Scrambled eggs, griddled
      asparagus and salmon on
      toast 171
Soft polenta with mushrooms
      and spinach 54
Solo chicken with rosemary
      and Roseval potatoes 130
soups
   All-round chicken soup 102–3
   Courgette soup with tarragon
      93
   Marcella's sugo 112–13
   Miso soup with noodles,
      shiitake mushrooms,
      spinach and an egg 32
   Roasted squash and carrot
      soup 106–7
   Spicy lentil soup with yoghurt
      and rocket 66
   Sweet potato soup with
      coconut and fresh coriander
      53
   10-minute pho 132

soy sauce
   Best-ever fried rice 71
   Bowl of rice with Chinesey
      vegetables 96
   Chinese egg noodles with
      steak and oyster sauce 73
   Cold noodle salad with
      cucumber and sashimi
      salmon 74
   Surinamese masala chicken
      118
   10-minute pho 132
spaghetti
   Pasta aglio olio my way 84
   Ridiculously easy spaghetti
      caprese 34
   Spaghetti with cherry
      tomatoes, nutmeg and
      ricotta 88
Spicy lamb pittas with hummus
      and garlicky yoghurt 30
Spicy lentil soup with yoghurt
      and rocket 66
spinach
   Miso soup with noodles,
      shiitake mushrooms,
      spinach and an egg 32
   Soft polenta with mushrooms
      and spinach 54
spring onions
   Best-ever fried rice 71
   Oatmeal congee 166
   10-minute pho 132
squash
   Roasted squash and carrot
      soup 106–7
steak
   Chinese egg noodles with
      steak and oyster sauce 73
   Good old steak sandwich 47
   Steak Béarnaise with chips
      and salad 124–5
   Steak tartare 139
stews
   Comforting little casseroles
      104–5
   Pork loin stewed with red
      wine and bay leaves 111

Stir-fried prawns with harissa
      mayo 172
sugar snap peas
   Chinese egg noodles with
      steak and oyster sauce 73
sugo, Marcella's 112–13
Surinamese masala chicken
      118
sweet potatoes
   Baked sweet potato with
      olives, feta and chilli 50
   Sweet potato soup with
      coconut and fresh coriander
      53

T
Tagliatelle with prawns and
      smoky whisky-tomato sauce
      41
Taleggio cheese
   Parma ham-Taleggio toastie
      de luxe 169
tapas 178
tarragon
   Courgette soup with tarragon
      93
tartlets
   Warm apple tartlet with
      vanilla ice cream 152
10-minute pho 132
Tenderstem broccoli
   Orecchiette with Tenderstem
      broccoli, anchovies and
      fennel seed 90
thyme
   Lamb chops with red wine
      and thyme sauce and green
      beans 138
Tiramisu for one 163
toast
   Parma ham-Taleggio toastie
      de luxe 169
   Scrambled eggs, griddled
      asparagus and salmon on
      toast 171
tomatoes
   Cassoulet 131
   Cheat's pizza Margherita 128

Chilli con everything 100
Cod in ginger-tomato sauce
    with gremolata and rice 68
A kind of pisto Manchego 29
Lemon couscous with salmon
    and cherry tomatoes 42
Marcella's sugo 112–13
Pasta sauce with fresh
    sausage and fennel seeds
    110
Polenta pizza with blistered
    cherry tomatoes and
    anchovies 57
Pork loin stewed with red
    wine and bay leaves 111
Ratatouille 116–17
Ridiculously easy spaghetti
    caprese 34
Spaghetti with cherry
    tomatoes, nutmeg and
    ricotta 88
Tagliatelle with prawns and
    smoky whisky-tomato sauce
    41
Warm lentil salad with grilled
    goat's cheese 64
Too-good-to-share cheese
    fondue 142
tuna
    Griddled white tuna with
        cucumber, avocado and
        ginger salad 38
    Salad of butter beans, tinned
        tuna and shaved fennel 44

V
vegetables
    Ratatouille 116–17
    Too-good-to-share cheese
        fondue 142
    see also peppers, tomatoes
        etc
vermicelli
    10-minute pho 132

W
Warm apple tartlet with vanilla
    ice cream 152

Warm salad of new potatoes
    and peppered mackerel 86
whisky
    Tagliatelle with prawns and
        smoky whisky-tomato sauce
        41
wine
    Cassoulet 131
    Lamb chops with red wine
        and thyme sauce and green
        beans 138
    Oysters, Champagne and a
        good book 181
    Pasta sauce with fresh
        sausage and fennel seeds
        110
    Pork loin stewed with red
        wine and bay leaves 111
    Tiramisu for one 163

Y
yoghurt
    Blackberry mess 146
    Pear-yoghurt swirl 160
    Spicy lamb pittas with
        hummus and garlicky
        yoghurt 30
    Spicy lentil soup with yoghurt
        and rocket 66

For me, myself and I

HQ
An imprint of HarperCollins*Publishers* Ltd
1 London Bridge Street
London SE1 9GF

10 9 8 7 6 5 4 3 2 1

First published in the Netherlands by Uitgeverij Podium 2016

First published in Great Britain by HQ
An imprint of HarperCollins*Publishers* Ltd 2017

ISBN 978-0-00-825667-8

Our policy is to use papers that are natural, renewable and recyclable products
and made from wood grown in sustainable forests. The logging and manufacturing
processes conform to the legal environmental regulations of the country of origin.

Photographs by Floortje van Essen-Ingen Housz

Printed and bound in Slovakia by Neografia a.s.